# Sparks In The Dark

WRITTEN BY CHRISTOPHER ROBERTSON AND THOMAS ROTELLA

Copyright © 2012 by Christopher Robertson and Thomas Rotella
First Edition – January 2012

**ISBN**
978-1-77097-058-8 (Hardcover)
978-1-77097-059-5 (Paperback)
978-1-77097-060-1 (eBook)

All rights reserved.

No part of this publication may be reproduced in any form, or by any means, electronic or mechanical, including photocopying, recording, or any information browsing, storage, or retrieval system, without permission in writing from the publisher.

These short stories are all works of fiction. All names, places and events are fictitious. Any resemblances to actual persons, places and events are completely coincidental, with the exception of "Welcome to the Jungle", all likenesses used by permission.

Published by:

**FriesenPress**
Suite 300 – 852 Fort Street
Victoria, BC, Canada V8W 1H8

www.friesenpress.com

Distributed to the trade by The Ingram Book Company

# Table of Contents

| | |
|---|---|
| Dedications | v |
| Foreward | vii |
| These Days | 1 |
| Knock, Knock | 11 |
| Boxed In | 19 |
| Sunshine on Chrome | 22 |
| A Sonnet For Jennifer | 41 |
| Cindy | 42 |
| The Little Things | 50 |
| Welcome To The Jungle | 65 |
| The Final Curtain | 75 |
| Joey : Part 1 | 78 |
| According To You | 81 |
| Hope | 85 |
| I Don't Love You Anymore | 91 |
| Lucky Socks | 95 |
| Joey : Part 2 | 117 |
| Coffee or Tea | 118 |
| The Job | 130 |
| Airplanes | 134 |
| Goodbye, My Love | 148 |
| Looking Back | 151 |
| 24 Hour Marathon | 159 |
| Drive | 171 |
| Better Than Dogs | 179 |
| Thicker Than Blood | 184 |
| Joey : Part 3 | 192 |
| The Promise | 194 |

# Dedications

**Chris**

Thanks,

*Mom,*
for encouraging me to read and be creative

*Phil,*
I love you bro

*Tom,*
For coming with me on this exciting journey
and the friendship that came with it

*Bruce,*
For the encouragement and just for being there

*Grant, Chris, Rene, Andy*
Friends like you guys are hard to find

*Lynn Wohlgemuth,*
For helping us through the process,

*The rest of my family and friends,*
You know who you are and what you mean to me

*Sean, Preston and Justyn,*
The three things I live and breathe for

*Jennifer,*
This life of mine can get pretty dark at times. You are always there to help me find my way. You are my strength, my rock, my spark. I love you.

***Tom***

With Love and Thanks

*To my mother Mary and father Sam,*
For creating and encouraging my imagination and passion for literature.

*To my sister Stephanie,*
For always being there, no matter what.

*To my family and friends,*
For their love and support.

*To Chris,*
For his friendship, his criticism and for the conversation that started it all.

*And to Crystal,*
For the kick in the ass and the constant motivation to strive for more.

You've been my own "spark in the dark", picking me up whenever I stumbled, and seeing in me things that I did not and sometimes still do not see.

No one in my life could possibly have done more for me than you.

# Foreward

*By Tom*

The story behind this book's completion was like any other white-knuckled tale you've heard. It was a dark and stormy night…the lightning cracked, lighting up the midnight sky, the thunder boomed, shaking the ground around us…the dark engulfed and swall…alright, that's all a lie.

We were working the day shift at our local grocery store like always. Shooting the shit like we always do. Conversations about films we've seen and movies we wanted to see. Books we've read and books we wanted to read. But on this particular day something was different.

Mr. Robertson brought an interesting topic to the table. He mentioned how (aside from films and reading) much he desired to write a novel. How he had so many ideas for stories colliding off one another in his head and how great they would be to get down on paper. I (Mr. Rotella) concurred immediately, admitting my own passion and desire to be on a shelf next to authors we've grown up reading.

And then, one day, something was brought to our attention. The Toronto Star and the city of Toronto were hosting a short story contest within the province of Ontario. For us it was a sign. We're both huge fans of the work by Stephen King, and more specifically, his short stories. To be able to sit down with a coffee and a book, and to be able to finish several different stories in that book before your coffee's even finished, well, it was something special. And we wanted it. So without delay, we set to work at creating our own short story to submit. The results? Christopher wrote the story The Promise, a story about a former gambler who wakes up to find himself in not-so-familiar territory, and I submitted Drive, a short about an ignorant, newly-turned sixteen-year old who wants more than anything to get behind the wheel of a car. Needless to say, neither of us won. But it did so much more for the two of us. We had been bitten by the writing bug. Bitten by the short story bug, to be more precise. And it took hold of us. It was at that moment that we began throwing ideas off one another and then turning them into words on our computer screens.

And what to do with those words? What to do with those finished products? Well, another fun-filled morning at work one day Chris provided the answer. Self-publishing. We both had dreams of sitting on a shelf next to someone like Mr. King, and thought this would be the way to do it. So we kept writing. We saved our money. Chris did more research than a mad scientist trying to make the dead rise. And then he came across the self-publishing company called FriesenPress. And he spoke with a woman there named Lynn Wohlgemuth, and she took us through the process. It was also with her help and guidance that this book came to life, and much thanks needs to be given to her.

When it came time to name our book, we bounced a few different titles, nothing really clicking for us. And one day Chris had a big smile on his face. "Why?" I asked. He said "I've got a name." I said "What is it?" He smiled again and said "Sparks in the Dark." I said "Hmmm." Not because I didn't like it. I did indeed like it. But I wasn't blown away by it. That is, until a couple minutes later, when he explained how he got it.

You see, Stephen King is a huge inspiration to the two of us. His short stories are pure brilliance. And in the Introduction of his book, Skeleton Crew, he says "Reading a good long novel is in many ways like having a long and satisfying affair...", before going on to say 'A short story is like a quick kiss in the dark from a stranger." We agree with Mr. King when he says that he writes short stories because they're a dying art form, and he wants to keep that art from "the lip of the drop into extinction's pit." And we want our book to be like that quick kiss, readers. That spark you feel when your lips touch, while everything around you is swallowed by the dark. We want you to feel that same spark as you take in every page. That spark of sadness. Laughter. Suspense. Horror. The spark that makes you want to turn the page, excited and hungry for more. And for that, Chris' title is pure genius.

And now the book is here, and you (the reader) are possibly sitting down, curled up on the couch, in bed or on a park bench, reading our very first book. A collaboration of short stories. And we'll let you in on something, dear readers. What a feeling. What a rush. It's been one hell of a ride for the two of us. There have been roadblocks, of course. Delays, self-criticism and the occasional writer's block. But the reward of having finished and being able to see someone holding it in their hands makes every moment worthwhile.

So we'd also like to thank all you readers out there. We've done our best to create a world for you and fill it with events and characters you may ultimately connect with or even despise. We're just glad that you decided to stop by for a visit.

# These Days

*By Chris*

The alley was dark, save for a glow of light coming from a trashcan sitting in the middle of the blackness. Walking closer, Rick could see the forms around the base of the can in the darkness. Three of them, all as close as they could get to the can without touching it. As he approached, he began to feel the heat emanating from the area.

One of the forms stirred on the ground. Rick looked down and saw that it was Louis. He carefully moved between Louis and the others to come up next to the can. He set down the sack he had been carrying, opened it, and pulled out a couple pieces of wood. Reaching in, he gently placed the wood onto the glowing embers so as not to send sparks everywhere, but also to stay quiet. Within a minute he had flames roaring. The heat coming off the can increased and he smiled.

Rick looked around and saw what he wanted over against the wall. He walked over, picked up a milk crate and went back to the barrel. Setting it down, he sat upon it, using it as a makeshift chair.

Louis, Heidi and Vince. They were the three forms lying around the barrel. He had come to know them over the last year or so. He lived in the building on the south side of the alley and had frequently seen them out here.

One day when it was especially cold out, he convinced his wife Karen to make a pot of soup. When it was done, it was then scooped into three bowls, and he took it down to the alley. They had thanked him for the soup and devoured it heartily, even waving up to the window in which Karen was looking out at them. Rick had sat with them a moment, chatting, getting to know their names, and then retreated back into the house. That was eleven months ago.

Since that time, many meals had been shared, much wood had been brought, and their stories had been told.

Rick looked down at Louis and recalled his story as it was told to him.

* * *

Louis was eight when his father had passed away. That had left Louis' mother with a lot of bills and no one to help her raise her two children, Louis and his older brother Dan. His mother had had to take on a second job in order to be able to provide for her boys. That left Louis and ten year old Danny to fend for themselves most of the time.

They never wanted for anything, there was always plenty of food in the house, a little money for them for an allowance, there was just never very much time. The boys adapted well, excelling in school, having lots of friends, but mostly they had each other.

Until the day Danny died.

Danny was fifteen, Louis thirteen. They had been playing football in the street with some of the neighborhood kids. The pass had come to Louis, but it was out of his reach and he had tipped it up into the air. Being the better athlete, Danny managed to grab it from the air and run.

That was the moment that Stephen Drees, in a drunken stupor, decided to ignore the stop sign in front of him. The car had hit Danny with such force that his shoes were actually left at the intersection where he was hit. His body was dragged for a full block underneath the car, until Mr. Drees had gone off the road and hit a tree.

Mr. Drees wound up serving only eight months in prison, but Louis was serving a life sentence of guilt.

If only he had caught the ball.

If only he hadn't tipped it into the air.

If only.

The incident was more than his mother could bear and just two months after Danny's death, she had killed herself. She had tried to kill Louis too, but was unsuccessful.

She had made Louis what she called a "special" drink. She sat him down at the table and told him not to get up until the drink was gone. Then she excused herself and said she was going to take a bath.

Louis sat at the table. He tasted the drink, and finding it horrible, he snuck over to the sink and dumped it out while he could still hear his mom's bathwater running. He returned to his seat and waited.

He heard the water stop running in the bathroom, and in its place he could hear her crying. He continued to sit there for a while, and eventually fell asleep waiting for her to come out.

When he woke, he had gone into the bathroom to make sure everything was OK, and that was when he found her. Her wrists and thighs had been cut open, and his father's straight razor was on the edge of the tub.

When the authorities arrived, they discovered that she had tried to make him drink antifreeze, thinking this would kill him while she offed herself in the tub.

He had gone to live with his Aunt Carol, his mother's sister, after the death of his mother. He was welcomed into the home with open arms.

Carol had two sons who were both older than Louis. John and Terry. They were seventeen year old twins. At first they left Louis alone but eventually they hauled him out of his shell and took him under their wing in the new neighborhood. They introduced him around to their friends and although he mostly felt like the odd man out, everyone seemed to welcome him graciously.

One night they were out with their friends, hanging out in what was affectionately known as "The Shack". Really it was just an old tree house in one of the kid's yards but by not calling it that they felt like it was still a cool place to hang out.

One of the boys they hung with, Dennis, never liked Louis from the day they had met. After being there for a while, Dennis had started to pick on Louis about his mother. Saying it was his fault she had died, and that he may as well have slit her wrists himself. Already saddled with the guilt of his brother's death, Louis snapped.

Louis claims that he doesn't remember exactly what happened, but he said the next thing he knew he was looking down from the tree house at Dennis' broken body.

Louis ran. He ran home, it was only a block away, grabbed a few things, raided the twins' money stash, took all the cash from Aunt Carol's purse, and then ran again. He wound up taking a bus to New York, and that is where, these days, he is still living.

* * *

Rick again looked down at Louis as his eyes filled with tears. Here was a young man, beaten and ravaged by guilt, but Rick could only do so much to help. Thinking of Louis' story only made him appreciate more the fact that his brother and mother were still alive and well.

Rick shivered. Realizing the fire was dying again, he bent down, grabbed a couple more pieces of wood, and placed them inside.

He looked up at the window to his apartment. He knew Karen was sleeping peacefully inside. He should be too, but tonight was one of the nights where sleep evaded him. It was these nights that he came down to make sure his friends were OK down here.

*Friends.*

Yes, if asked he would say he considered these three his friends.

Vince stirred and sat up. Looking around, he spied Rick.

"Can't sleep tonight Rick?" Vince asked.

"No, she's being a tricky beast to catch tonight." Rick replied.

Vince laughed as he laid his head back down and fell back asleep.

* * *

There wasn't much to tell as far as Vince was concerned.

He was a newlywed when his story begins. He had a beautiful wife. (She really was, Rick had seen photos.) A new home, new car and money in the bank. Vince worked at a very successful investment firm, while his wife Sabrina also had a job that she loved.

One morning over breakfast Sabrina had told Vince she was pregnant. Vince had been overjoyed. He had always wanted a family and so had she. Vince had tried to convince her that they should both take the day off to celebrate, but she had insisted that they go to work and celebrate later that night. He reluctantly agreed but went to work happy. He had spent the drive to work riding on a silver cloud. When he arrived he bragged to everyone who would listen that he was going to be a father.

Then it happened.

At around nine o'clock word began to trickle in of the attack. At ten after, word of the second attack came and Vince's whole world shattered. It was September eleventh, two thousand one. Sabrina worked at the World Trade Center, and in the span of about twenty minutes, Vince had lost everything.

Two months later he found his way to this alley, and also to Louis.

\* \* \*

Rick again looked up to his apartment window, and thanked God that he still had the woman he loved. They had spent over fifty years together. Sure there had been hardships, some that even threatened to put them in a similar situation to the one his friends here found themselves in. He believed it was perseverance and their love for each other was what had led them through.

Rick looked at his watch. Two thirty. He stooped over and grabbed the last of the wood, placing it in the barrel. He could feel himself starting to get tired but he wasn't quite ready to head inside yet.

He sat back down.

Reaching into his pocket, he pulled out a pack of cigarettes and a lighter. Of all the things he had given up over the years, this had to be the most difficult. He had actually managed to quit for over twenty years, but once retired he picked them back up. He had assumed it was out of boredom. He only smoked a couple a day, mostly just for something to do but sometimes when he was deep in thought.

Looking at the two men and the woman lying on the ground in front of him, he lit his cigarette. The warmth from the fire felt good. He looked down at Heidi. Hers was the smallest of the three shapes, but hers was also the saddest story to recall.

When they had first met, Rick had judged her to be in her late forties or early fifties, and was shocked to find out she was only eighteen.

\* \* \*

Heidi had gotten on a bus in her hometown of Omaha, Nebraska with her parents blessing. She had decided to come to New York to seek her fame and fortune in music or movies. Her parents loved her dearly, so instead of losing her to arguments and fights, they decided to embrace her decision and help her in any way they could. They had purchased her ticket, gave her money, and even arranged for a small apartment to move into when she got there.

Heidi had settled in, and after two weeks had found a job waiting on tables in a little diner down the street from her apartment. She worked mostly afternoon and night shifts which left her day open to go chasing down agents and contacts.

One night while working, she was talking to one of the other girls about trying to find new contacts when a young man sitting nearby called her over.

"Excuse me." He said as she came over.

"What can I do for you, sweetie?" She asked.

"Listen, I couldn't help but overhear your conversation, and I think this might be your lucky day."

"Oh yeah, how's that?" She asked, rolling her eyes.

He reached into his pocket, pulled out his wallet, and handed her a card.

*Reid Smith, Photographer.*

She looked down at the man sitting in the booth. "Photographer, huh?"

"Yup."

"Well Mr. Uhh.." She looked at the card. "Well Mr. Smith, just because you are a photographer, I don't see how this makes it my lucky day."

"Let me photograph you."

Heidi laughed. "I ain't got no money to be wasting it on that type of thing." She set his card on the table and turned to walk away.

"Wait, what if I told you I didn't want any money."

She turned back. "I'd ask you where you got the drugs," she laughed.

"But I really don't want any money from you."

"What, you just go around working for free? That's mighty Samaritanish' of you."

"No, I don't work for free. I get paid by the agents who sign the girls I photograph."

"How's that?" She asked.

"I'm like a talent scout. I guess. I find the girls, take their photos, and hand them in. If the agents like the photos, they call you. If they end up signing you, I get a percentage."

Intrigued by what the young man was saying, she sat down in the booth with him. They talked for a while longer, and she had agreed to let him photograph her. They were to meet her at her apartment when she got off work and they would do the photos there.

When she arrived at home she found him to be waiting out front for her, sitting on her steps with a duffle bag at his feet. She brought him inside and helped him set up his equipment.

They hung a white sheet on the living room wall to use as a backdrop. Setting up his tripod, he told her to go into her closet to find some clothes that she would like to be photographed in.

After selecting her clothes and changing into one of the outfits, she came out of the bedroom to find him sitting at the table waiting for her. He was drinking a bottle of water. When she walked over, he grabbed another bottle of water off the table and handed it to her.

"I hope you don't mind." He said as he drank. "I went in your fridge and got these. I thought you might be thirsty too."

"No it's fine," she said as she took a long swallow from the bottle handed to her.

They went into the living room and she began to pose as he started taking pictures. After coming from the bedroom from changing again, he handed her another water. She drank this one down in one shot, and then excitedly took her place in front of the sheet. After fifteen minutes or so she had started to become dizzy and the world drifted away into a fog.

When she regained her senses hours later she found herself face down on the floor. Realizing she was nude she grabbed the sheet which was now lumped on the floor beside her and covered herself up.

Sitting in the middle of the room, she looked around. Everything was a mess. Her entire apartment had been torn apart, and from where she sat it looked like everything that was worth anything had been taken.

She stood slowly, and made her way around the apartment. Every room was in the same disorder. Things were either missing or broken. Even her bed, pillows, couch and chair had all been cut open and relieved of their stuffing. She sat back down on the living room floor, looking at her purse, the contents of which were scattered all over the room. Except for her wallet and cell phone, which were both missing.

She was about to get up when her eye caught a glimpse of something under the corner of the couch. It was a camera. She knew as she picked it up that it wasn't hers. It must have been his. Thinking some of the pictures on it may give a clue as to where he lived, she turned it on and began to scroll through the pictures stored on it.

The images flicking across the tiny screen were horrible. They were pictures of two men engaged in all kinds of lewd acts with a woman. Sometimes just one but most times it was both men. Seeing the birthmark on the inside of the woman's thigh brought the realization that she was looking at pictures of herself.

She forced herself to look at the complete set of pictures, so she could see everything that had been done to her. All the while wondering to herself, how could this have happened, when suddenly it dawned on her.

*The water.*

Both times he had handed her a bottle of water, they had already been opened.

She was crying now as she looked at the photos of herself being raped. But not just raped, absolutely violated in every way possible. It was like watching a hardcore porn slideshow. At one point both men were standing above her, urinating on her face.

She screamed and threw the camera across the room. She was weak and the camera fell short of the wall and skidded harmlessly across the floor. She got up, still keeping the sheet around her and made her way to the door. She would go next door and use the neighbor's phone.

Just before she reached the door, it swung open on her and standing there was the photographer, Reid Smith. She was about to scream when he quickly rushed forward and grabbed her by the throat. Without saying a word, he kicked the door shut behind him.

Reaching behind, he pulled a knife seemingly from nowhere and held it up for her to see. His hand still on her throat, squeezing tightly he backed her up to the couch. She had almost tripped as the sheet fell away while backing up. Pinning her against the back of the couch, he lowered the knife and then suddenly thrust it forward, stabbing her in the belly.

She tried to scream but couldn't as he still held tight to her throat. He stabbed her once more in the belly and then threw her down to the floor. The last thing she remembered was his boot coming down onto her face.

She woke two days later in the hospital. Turns out the stab wounds had missed hitting anything important. So her belly was OK. Her face on the other hand was another story.

After he stomped her unconscious, he had decided to take the knife to her face. The police believed the only reason she hadn't died was because a neighbor had come by, saw her door was open, and found her lying in a pool of blood.

The mess he had made of her face had required over four hundred stitches to repair. The doctors had told her that she was going to require numerous plastic surgeries, but stated that she would always have the scars from the attack.

She walked away from the hospital that night, still wrapped in the bloody bandages.

Two days after that she had shown up in the alley.

* * *

Rick looked at the young girl as tears rolled down his aged cheeks. He stood, stretched, and walked away from the fire. He made his way down the alley, into his building, and up into his apartment.

When he climbed into bed Karen rolled over and looked at him.

"What?" He asked.

"Nothing," she said with a smile.

"It must be something if you're smiling like that."

"I just can't believe that I am married to such a wonderful, caring man."

"Aww shucks, lady," he joked.

"I'm serious. You have been taking care of those people for almost a year now, never asking for anything in return. And you still have enough love left for me."

Rick smiled. ""I really do love you."

"I know." Karen replied. "I love you too."

She hugged him and they settled down to sleep.

* * *

Karen died that night while sleeping in her husband's arms.

That was two weeks ago.

\* \* \*

These days there are four people sleeping by the fire in the alley.

# Knock, Knock

*By Tom*

"Max, shutup!"

The little Jack Russell Terrier's barks immediately ceased, replaced by a steady stream of whimpering, which was then punctuated by the occasional look of reproach at its master.

Jared Stokes moved past the small ball of fury to the front door, pressed his face to the window and peered outside.

Darkness.

With the streetlamps having burnt out a few weeks ago and the cloud-covered sky providing no moonlight from above, it was next to impossible for Jared to figure out what had been making Max go nuts for the last twenty minutes.

"Go lie down, boy," he said gently, ushering the dog away from the door.

Jared made his way back into the kitchen, removed a box of biscuits from the cupboard and tossed a treat to the four-legged soldier at his feet.

"There you go, big man," he said, watching Max chomp down greedily on his cookie. "Now can I please get back to my night?"

He put the box back on the shelf, closed the door and sighed.

Friday nights had become something of a ritual with Jared lately.

A couple months ago (on a Friday night to be exact), Jared's girlfriend of four years had handed back her promise ring and called the relationship off, claiming "she needed time to think."

Apparently, Jared had been asleep for the second part of that conversation, where she had gone on to say "…HAHAHA…you're an idiot."

Less than a week later, she had found herself attached to the arm of a new guy, this one complete with a fake tan, bigger muscles and a mirror and comb in his back pocket.

Yes, she was moving up in the world.

*Not like I can talk*, Jared thought, scooping generous amounts of Heavenly Hash ice cream into a bowl.

Since then, Jared had spent every Friday night curled up on the couch with movies, Max, and an endless supply of food.

Tonight's raison d'être: The Simpsons. Season Seven. On DVD.

Jared's family hadn't really been of any help to the situation.

His mother had told him to smarten up, saying, "You're only 19, you don't even know what love is yet."

In a poorly executed manner, Jared had foolishly retaliated with "… says the divorced mother of two."

His mother still wasn't speaking to him.

And then there was his sister, whose only means of solace was to repeatedly call him an idiot.

He had it somewhere in the area of sixty.

So here he was again.

The infamous Friday night.

Homer, Bart and the gang were his friends and confidants.

The only difference tonight was that Jared had the house entirely to himself.

His mother had flown to Hawaii for two weeks with a small group of friends; and his sister, tasting freedom from rules and curfews, had called up her friends immediately.

*Knock, knock.*

Jared jumped, his heart skipping a few extra beats, not only by the sound at the door, but by Max's immediate outburst of barking.

"Max, quiet!" he snapped, regaining his composure and making his way to the door.

Moving the dog aside gently with his foot, Jared flipped one of the light switches on in the hall and watched as the front porch lit up.

Looking through the glass of the front door, he saw nothing outside.

Unlocking the bolt, Jared swung the door open slowly, attempting to get a better look.

He scanned what he could of the front yard and driveway, but the rays of the porch light extended as far as the stairs where the porch itself ended.

The darkness around him suddenly unnerved him, the way it consumed everything around him, threatened to engulf the remaining light around him.

Scolding himself for letting his nerves intimidate the rest of him, Jared locked the screen door, closed the big door, relocked it and went back to the couch.

"Just relax, Max," he said with a mouthful of ice cream, as he watched the dog sitting upright and alert, a low growl emanating from within him. "You're making me nervous."

*Knock, knock.*

Jared jumped again, almost choking on the frozen dessert.

He quickly stood up, his heart racing a little faster than he cared to admit, and ran back to the front door.

The lights still shone on the porch, giving him a clear view of the jackass outside.

Within seconds, he felt his insides twisting and turning, a bead of sweat forming and slipping down his forehead.

No one there.

*Dammit*, he thought.

*How did they disappear so fast?* He wondered nervously.

The distance between the couch and door was smaller than that of the door to the stairs of the porch, Jared would have seen someone.

Unless they hopped over the rail.

His nerves rattled, he opened the front door, put his hands on the screen door and strained to see into the darkness.

"Who's there?" he called, his voice breaking slightly.

The eerie, pitch black silence was his only reply.

Quickly, Jared stepped back, slammed the door closed and bolted both locks.

He stood there a moment, thinking hard, before finally making a decision.

Ignoring the growls of the dog at his feet, Jared walked into the kitchen, picked up the phone on the wall by the sink, and dialled his sister's cell phone.

After half a dozen rings, she finally picked up.

"This better be good Jar-head. I'm at the show."

Jared scowled at his sister's attitude.

"Jess, can you please come home?"

Silence on the other line. "Can I please come home?" she repeated slowly. "Did you not just hear me tell you I'm out?"

"Jess I wouldn't ask unless I thought it was important."

"OK," she replied quickly. "So why's it important?"

Jared thought the question over, wondering how much to tell her. He decided it was all or nothing.

"Somebody's screwing with me," he said.

Again, silence from his sister.

"What do you mean, somebody's screwing with you?" she asked. "Like prank calling the house?"

"No. They're knocking on the front door. Both times I looked outside, nobody was there. Max is going nuts."

The sounds on the other line were muffled, but he thought he could make out the sounds of laughter.

"OK," his sister finally said. "Let me get this straight. Somebody's knocking on the door and running away, and wee wittle Jared is getting scared?"

Jared felt his face getting red with anger as he listened to his sister taunt him, no doubt in front of all her friends.

"Jared, you do know what a teenager is, right?" she continued, clearly enjoying herself. "You're aware this is the kind of stuff we teenagers do? Prank calling, throwing eggs, knocking on doors, throwing timbits at people from our cars? Any of it ring a bell?"

Jared attempted to keep himself from losing his temper.

"I'm aware, thanks. I just thought it would be better if you came home is all."

His sister was laughing freely now, clearly not concerned with hiding it.

"So I can save you from the boogeyman, big bro? That it?"

"Forget it," Jared snapped. "Forget I asked."

"Well c'mon, Jared," she replied quickly. "You're acting like you just bi-passed teenager and detoured right back to child years, complete with Mom checking the closet and under your bed."

Feeling his face growing hot with embarrassment, Jared made no attempt to reply.

"Does this have anything to do with Miss Horsefacedslutbag? Stop being an idiot, Jared. Get over the bitch."

Sixty one.

"Great advice from the love doctor," Jared spat at the phone. "You and mom should teach classes. How to be alone the rest of your lives. And who knows, maybe you can even teach a major in how to stay a virgin until you're 50."

Click.

Jared smiled.

If anything, Jared had succeeded in not only getting the last word in, but also enraging his sister.

KNOCK, KNOCK.

The sounds were louder this time, causing Jared to drop the phone and Max to bark insanely.

"Son of a bitch!" he yelled.

As he turned to run to the front door, Jared's eyes caught sight of the knife rack next to the oven, six black handles all sticking out into the air.

Grabbing the biggest blade in the rack, Jared made his way to the front entrance, unlocked both doors, and walked out onto the porch, the knife at his side.

"Who's there?" he called out to the darkness. "C'mon, come say hello!"

Silence.

Jared paced back and forth, making sure to stay in the vicinity of the light around him.

Suddenly the *SNAP* of a twig came to his right, in the front yard.

Jared's eyes scanned the darkness, seeing nothing but black, but feeling the hair on his arms rise at who or what was out there.

CRUNCH.

The other sound came from his left, from the driveway, as though someone had put a foot down and twisted it into the gravel and stones.

Fear gripped him at what he couldn't see.

He would have preferred to have a glimpse at what was out there.

Preferred to see what taunted him from the dark abyss.

What was coming at him.

This was worse.

And what made it more terrifying was that he had the feeling of eyes on him.

Watching him from the dark.

Reading the fear in his eyes.

The knife in his hand shook.

He looked over to the door.

Max stood there, his back paws on the floor, his front paws on the screen door, barking into the night.

Five feet, he judged.

That was all he had to run.

He hesitated.

Frozen.

Another branch snapped under the weight of an unseen foot.

He ran.

Refused to look behind him.

Grabbed the handle on the screen door.

Jumped inside and locked both doors.

Breathing heavily, Jared slumped to the floor.

Max sat by his side, licking his hand.

A minute or two passed.

Some Friday night.

Getting slowly to his feet, Jared came to a sudden decision.

Call the police.

He ran back to the phone in the kitchen.

Somebody wanted to screw with him, let them answer to the cops.

See how tough they were then.

THUD!

Jared spun, as something connected with the kitchen window.

Knife in hand, he ran back to the door to see what had hit the window.

SMASH!

The light on the porch went out, shattered and expelled by whatever had hit it.

Now Jared had no light.

Nothing but darkness surrounded him.

THUD! THUD! THUD!

The sounds came from all around him, hitting every side of the house.

Max had stopped barking, running into the living room and hiding under the coffee table.

*THUD! THUD! THUD!*

"Leave me alone!" he shouted from inside the house. "Just leave me alone!"

*THUD!*

"Damn you!" he screamed.

Before he knew what he was doing, Jared had unlocked the doors, and ran into the darkness.

"Where are you?!" he shouted, running through the front yard. "Show yourself!"

He could barely make out his own hand in front of his face.

But he continued to run wildly, rage pumping through him, engulfing his body and mind faster than the darkness around him could.

He stopped at the side of the house, struggling to see or hear something. Anything.

The silence that answered was more menacing than actually hearing something.

He continued to run, stopping to unlock the gate leading into the back yard.

He heard a sound behind him.

Turning, he heard footsteps coming at him.

Without thinking, he thrust the knife out in front of him.

Felt something's weight run straight into it.

Felt the blade pierce into flesh.

Felt the whoosh of air escape its lips as the life was drained from it.

Jared let go of the knife as the body went limp and fell to the ground.

Suddenly he heard another sound behind him.

He turned around.

Saw a light dancing in the dark toward him.

Heard a voice ring out:

"Rachel? Rachel? Where are you?"

That voice.

"Who's there?" he called out, his voice weak.

"Jared?" it replied. 'Is that you?"

The light made its way onto his face.

"Jared?"

He strained his eyes.

"Jess?" he said.

His eyes adjusting to the light, Jared noticed the shocked yet satisfied smile on his sister's face.

Saw the flashlight in her left hand.

Saw the balloons in her right.

Water balloons.

"You?" he cried. "You did this?"

She smiled.

"Me and Rachel," she said happily. "Joke's on you, eh?"

"Rachel…" Jared began faintly.

He looked into his sister's face, as the beam of the flashlight moved past him.

Saw her smile disappear.

Saw the look of horror creeping out of every crevasse of her face.

Watched the flashlight bounce up and down in shock.

Jared didn't look back, knowing what lay behind him.

"Joke's on me," he said softly.

# Boxed In

*By Tom*

They've come with weapons.

Fire burning in their eyes, I feel them searching for me.

Yelling and cursing, they smash and slam against the glass, trying to get to me.

I pinch my arm. Maybe I'm stuck in a dream.

I feel my nails dig into the flesh of my arm.

Not dreaming.

I look back at them, hoping they're not there, a hallucination.

"Just make it easier on yourself buddy! C'mon out!" one of them yells.

Not a hallucination.

This was supposed to be an easy job.

No danger.

Work alone.

Good pay.

I want to strangle the asshole who hired me.

The only reason they haven't already put a bullet in my head is the three-inch thick pane of bullet resistant glass.

Now they're pounding on the high performance bolted door, the clubs pounding relentlessly upon it.

How much time do I have until they're through?

It can't be much.

A shiver flows through me, even though the temperature in the room is unreasonably high.

I'm stuck in a giant safe, and the only way out is through them.

I know this.

They know this.

I feel the beads of sweat – or is it tears? – clinging to my face.

Looking around, I see nothing that will help me out of this.

The safe is at my feet, spilling its treasures all over the floor.

There are papers, pens, pencils and other tools scattered about the desk.

A phone sits in the corner.

Who would I even call?

No one can help me.

I'm alone.

Boxed in.

Completely screwed.

I kick the chair away, and sit down cross-legged on the floor to escape from the ceaseless pounding.

I cover my ears and close my eyes, dropping my head to face the ground.

Hopeless.

Running my hands through my hair, I look over at the safe.

At this level, I see something wedged in between the underside of the desk and the top of the safe.

Reaching into the dark gap, I feel my hands close over something.

It's cool to the touch.

Before I even pull my hand back out, I know what it is.

Withdrawing my hand, I switch the loaded firearm into my right hand, working it in like a kid with his brand new baseball glove.

My mind starts to clear.

These monsters want me to surrender.

I will not surrender.

I will not pray.

I will not beg for wings.

The one-way mirror finally cracks under the hundredth swing of their clubs.

I rise to my feet, my finger on the trigger.

These men try to cast me into the dark.

I have been given a light.

They've tried to end my story.

I am holding the end to theirs.

In life, the only way to overcome chaos is to create more of it.

On the other side of the glass, the men pause in their activity, as one pulls out a ringing phone.

"Yes, we're almost in," he says into it. "But he's not cooperating."

A pause as the man listens to someone on the other line.

"Yes sir," he finally says. "It'll be over in two minutes."

Closing the phone, he puts it back in his pocket, pulls his gun out and aims it at the window.

"Last offer pal! You have one minute to come out with your hands up, or we will use force to remove you!"

I smile.

Come and get me coppers.

# Sunshine on Chrome

### *By Tom*

His name was David Legault.

He told me to call him Dave.

His friends all called him Black Ice.

But now, as I stared into those once warm and friendly eyes, I admit I did not recognize the man who looked back into mine.

The mask had been lifted and the true face was exposed.

And it terrified me.

So I prayed.

I prayed like I have never prayed before.

* * *

It had all started my first year of college.

We were all halfway through the semester, and I was on the path to what I hoped would become the city's next top cop.

But it was a road that I knew was bound to be roughly paved and difficult to navigate.

Nowadays, the career world had gone in a new direction.

It was now about the people you knew, not the knowledge you gained.

Total bullshit.

Guys and gals were getting hired because their family ties stretched far and high or because mom and dad occasionally had lunch with a CEO or some other top dog.

It was an unfair world to be sure, but I persisted nonetheless.

I had never been the kind of guy to slink away from a challenge and I wasn't about to start now.

Besides, Bradley Dunn was the kind of guy who always seemed to get what he wanted.

My teachers were awed by me.

My friends wanted to be me.

And the girls all wanted to be with me.

I never found myself lured into "gettin baked", or awoke one morning to find my arms wrapped around a toilet seat with a cartoon Popeye tattooed to my penis.

I had fun, but I always knew where to draw the line.

My parents were paying my tuition and rooming, all the while threatening to ask for back pay unless I made the honour roll, so I took my studies seriously.

I didn't have time for a relationship, but if the girl was willing to wake up the next morning to a handshake and a "thanks again", everything seemed to work out just fine.

And then I met Elizabeth Legault.

* * *

We met in the school's cafeteria one morning, as I skimmed through the display of overripe bananas, bruised apples and dried out oranges.

I saw her through a rack of mini cereal boxes, her face radiantly shining between the cardboard mugs of Tony the Tiger and Toucan Sam.

I had to talk to her, and from there it played out like a scene from The Notebook or some other Meet Cute moment.

I quickly (which in The Notebook would be slowed down dramatically) made my way over to her, pushing aside professors and fellow students to do so.

She was drop dead gorgeous.

Long, brown hair.

Big, chestnut eyes.

Her skin looked smooth and had a natural olive tint.

She had a tiny, cute-as-a-button nose and capped it all off with perfectly shaped lips.

She didn't show off the faultless curves of her body, but sweet Marybeth did she have them.

A girl like this deserved only the most charming, intellectual conversation a person could muster.

"H-Hi," I coughed.

She smiled back.

And just like that I was in.

We chatted a while.

She was polite.

So polite.

Polite to the point where I thought she was just having me on and at some point Ashton himself would come up behind me yelling "You just got Punk'd asshole!" And the two of them would high five and dance circles around me, rhyming with my name in a silly chant.

And I would cry.

And they would laugh.

But no!

She was just a genuinely nice girl who seemed to be genuinely interested in talking to me.

I discovered that she was also in her first year of college too.

Driving on an adjacent road of difficulty herself, studying to be an elementary school teacher.

Since both of us lived on campus, we decided to meet after dinner for a nice end-of-winter night walk and a coffee from Tim Hortons.

We were college students; it was the highest level of romance we could afford.

* * *

About a month later, the two of us were still bearing the marks from Cupid's bow.

We had breaks together.

We had lunch together.

We had dinner together.

We put on weight together.

We exercised together.

She was an innocent girl in all respects.

Sure, we had kissed and we had hugged.

But when she would ask me to "come over and watch a movie", to my bitter disappointment, I could recite every line back of Moulin Rouge when it was over.

I think one time her hand grazed the area very close to my crotch, but she pretended she was only recovering some dropped popcorn (which she was, but a graze is a graze).

No, she was twenty and still a virgin.

And I was fine with that.

Neither one of us had let the time we spent together interfere with our school work, but with spring break right around the corner, the two of us were eager to kick the books aside.

And then she dropped the bombshell.

The end credits had just begun to roll of another Oscar winner, when she slid two feet closer to me (yet still with two feet to go) and grabbed my hand.

"Yes, pretty lady?"

She smiled. Slid another foot closer.

"I have a question."

"I'm all ears."

She paused, biting her lip in a sort of *Should I ask him?* kind of way.

"Well," she said finally. "I was just wondering..."

*If i brought protection?*

*Fancied a tumble?*

*Was into three-ways?*

"I was wondering if you wanted to come home with me and meet my parents."

I choked and bit my tongue.

"Y-your parents?" I finally coughed out.

"It would only be a few days!" she cried, looking scared. "I'm sorry, I know it's too early, I just thou..."

"Hold on," I said, interrupting her quickly.

I hesitated, taking in her beauty as the glow from the television illuminated her face.

"It's fine," I said a moment later, smiling. "I would love to meet them."

She leaped the other foot into my arms and placed a dozen kisses on my lips and cheeks.

Then, smiling widely, she made her way back over to the other side of the couch.

* * *

Less than two weeks later, we were on the road, making the three-hour drive to her parents' house. The weekend after she had popped the question, I jumped on a bus home and borrowed my father's car.

We talked and laughed the whole drive up, broken up with fits of hysterical laughter as I attempted to mimic Aerosmith.

Around two in the afternoon, we pulled into the driveway of castle Legault.

I cast a nervous glance at the front window of the house, wondering if her father was standing just out of sight, rubbing his hands together and laughing maniacally , all the while muttering "fallen right into my trap…"

"You're going to be fine," she said, breaking me out of my slasher film. "They're going to love you."

I looked at her sceptically, said nothing and made my way out of the car.

She skipped to the front door, disappearing inside, while I slowly trailed behind.

Reaching the front porch, I was just preparing to call for Liz when a voice stopped me.

"So you're Brad," it said.

I looked up and screamed out in horror.

* * *

Alright I lied about the scream.

But if I had my voice when the door had opened I would have.

Her father was two streets past intimidating and one short of changing my boxer/briefs.

He was a grizzly bear of a man, somewhere around 6'3 and maybe 230 pounds.

He was bald on top and sported a brown moustache and beard, both of them with creeping greys.

He had the physique of a built man slightly past his prime, with a small beer belly protruding from the black Harley Davidson T-shirt.

The skin that was showing on him was completely covered in tattoos, from fanged spiders, menacing tigers and even a deadly snake that wound itself all the way up his arm to his shoulder.

Oh my.

I stood there, lost for words, as he looked straight through me with two, x-ray-capable, scrutinizing eyes.

"Mr. Legault," I whispered, terrified. "Very nice to meet you."

He took a step towards me.

"Nice to meet you son!" he cried, grabbing my hand in tight grip. "How was the drive?"

"Uhhhh...it...it was good."

"Good, good. Well, leave the bags, we'll get them later. Come on in and have a drink, Brad, don't be shy. And call me Dave."

And with a smile on his face and shocked relief on mine, he wrapped an arm around my back and swept me inside.

\* \* \*

It was nothing like I imagined.

Every ounce of dread I had bottled up on the ride over had all but evaporated and disappeared.

Dave and Linda Legault were exceptionally warm people.

After a quick introduction and rum and coke in their kitchen, they showed me downstairs to their guest bedroom, where I would *obviously* be sleeping alone.

And I was fine with that.

Minutes later, the four of us were talking out back on their patio, while Dave barbequed steaks and baked potatoes on the grill.

When dinner was over, the women went into the kitchen to wash dishes and I sat there alone with Dave, talking about his greatest passion: motorcycles.

"You want to see my Harley?" he asked, taking another sip of his Caesar.

"For God's sake, David, the boy's been on the road all morning, barely been in the house and you're already bothering him," Mrs. Legault called from the kitchen.

She appeared at the entrance of the dining room, dish towel over her shoulder and an exasperated expression on her face.

"Brad, I give you full permission to tell my husband to get a life. Honestly, the man has a sick obsession with his bike."

I smiled, looking over at Mr. Legault. He suddenly looked like a kid in a department store, who had picked up a new toy, asking mommy and daddy if he could take it home. How do you say no?

"It's not a problem, Mrs. Legault. I would love to see it sir."

Dave looked over at his wife, fixing her with a boyish grin that said, *Na na na na na na!*

She went back into the kitchen, rolling her eyes and smiling.

Dave jumped up from his chair and took one last gulp from his glass.

"To the garage, my boy!" he shouted, wiping his mouth with the back of his palm.

We made our way downstairs to the front hall, stopping next to a door across from the hall closet.

We slipped into our shoes and, Dave in lead, made our through the door and into the garage.

One look around told me that only one person was ever allowed in here.

The garage was cleaner than my family doctor's office, and my doctor was borderline OCD.

A small shelf took up part of the back wall, holding a few thingamabobs and whatchmacallits.

A giant tool chest sat in the far corner, two bicycles perched on their kickstands next to it.

And right in the middle of the spotless car hold was the Harley Davidson beauty.

Well, it was covered with a black tarp, but by the look Dave kept giving me as he prepared to throw the tarp back, I was about to be awed.

"You ready?" he asked, clearly excited.

I nodded. I would've said yes if it were a unicycle with training wheels.

He threw back the tarp, his eyes locked on my reaction.

I'll admit, my knowledge of bikes was limited.

Actually I know nothing of motorcycles.

At all.

But looking at the beast on two wheels in front of me, I was impressed.

It was a 2010 Dyna Wide Glide, Dave told me.

It was a solid, black with brilliant silver and orange flames.

But what really caught my attention was the chrome.

Chrome gleamed from every nook and cranny, from the tank to the handlebars.

"It's beautiful," I said, really meaning it.

Dave looked proudly back, smiling down at it, nodding in agreement.

"Yeah, she's my second child."

I laughed.

He didn't.

I stopped.

"I don't really know a lot about bikes," I told him, "but I'm diggin' the chrome."

He laughed, but looked thrilled by my observation.

"Are you? I'm glad you like it. Personally, there ain't nothing prettier in this world than sunshine on chrome."

I nodded silently, watching as the big man in front of me was practically melting at the bike's feet.

And that's when the realization hit me.

David Legault was no grizzly.

He was a giant teddy bear.

With tattoos.

* * *

That night, Liz and I were sitting in the living room, catching the last few minutes of a movie before we hit the hay.

"So," she began, avoiding my eyes.

"So," I replied, staring at the side of her head.

She looked uncomfortable, twitching in her seat, hands and arms unable to remain still.

"Well...what did you think?"

I looked back at her, looking politely confused.

"I'm sorry? Think of what?"

She turned her head, looking politely irritated.

Well, maybe not politely.

"Oh, c'mon Brad," she said, slapping my knee. "You know I mean my parents."

I laughed.

She didn't.

I stopped.

"Right. Your parents."

She continued to stare at me, hanging on to my every word as though I were explaining how to diffuse a bomb.

"I'll be honest, Liz," I said, straight faced. "I think they're monsters."

Her jaw dropped open, her shocked expression slowly transforming into anger.

"Excuse me?"

I sighed, thoroughly amused but concealing it well.

"Well, the way they keep your sister locked up in the garage day and night," I explained, "I'm a little shocked you don't say something."

Her lips, pulled tightly together, at once split apart as she broke into a fit of laughter.

"Not cool," she said, pretending to sucker punch me in the stomach.

I laughed, gently grabbing her fingers, placing a kiss on her tiny knuckles.

"I'm obviously kidding. I think they're fantastic."

"Really?"

"You bet," I said. "But I think each of us should go to bed now, don't you?"

"Why's that?" she asked, looking puzzled.

"Three reasons," I replied quietly. "It's late. I can almost hear your father pacing upstairs. And three...when he gets up at four a.m. to make his nightly check on his bike, I'd rather not die when he finds his other child down here with me."

She laughed. I didn't.

She continued to laugh anyways.

"Goodnight," she said.

Kissing me on the cheek, she quietly made her way upstairs.

\* \* \*

The week went better than I expected.

Dave and I bonded more than either of us probably anticipated, and spent more time together than Liz and I.

On our second last day before we left, Dave asked if I wanted to go for a drive, grab a coffee and meet a few of his friends.

After a nod and a thumb up from Liz, Dave and I were out of the driveway and on the road.

"So where are we meeting your friends?" I asked.

"Coffee shop a few minutes from here," he replied, head bobbing as Bob Marley sang Three Little Birds over the radio. "We usually meet a couple times a week, just to shoot the shit about the old days."

"How come you didn't take your bike?" I asked, looking out at the blue skies. "It's nice enough."

"It is," he replied, "and the guys will are probably riding theirs. But I've got a passenger with me today. And nobody's ass sits on my bike but mine."

A silent pause filled up the car before both of us broke into laughter.

A few minutes later, we pulled into the coffee shop's parking lot. At the back of the lot sat three other bikes.

Three men stood ten feet from them, each one with a lit cigarette sitting at the end of their fingertips.

After parking the car, Dave nodded to me and we both got out.

All three of the men stared at me, the new intruder into their midst.

"Hey assholes!" Dave shouted to them, making his way over to my side.

"Who's the kid?" One of them called back. He was tall and skinny with a ponytail, and looked like he had been cooked well done by the sun. "You in Big Brothers or something Davey boy?"

"This is Brad Dunn," Dave replied. "Lizzie's boyfriend."

The reaction was instant and simultaneous.

They all took a step closer, each one of the men's eyes narrowed, their faces immobile as they stared down at me.

"Easy, ladies," Dave cautioned, smiling. "He's a good boy."

Again the reaction was synchronized, all of them breaking into laughter.

"Sorry, bud," a hairy, muscular one said, holding out his hand. "We're just protective of little Lizzie."

I forced a laugh, swallowed the brief spell of fear and took the man's hand.

"I'm Bubba," he said, almost breaking my fingers in his grasp.

"Sideshow," said the tall one.

"Buck," said the third, a heavyset man with no hair save for the long, grey beard hanging from his face.

Like Dave, all three men were covered head to foot in tattoos; and, like Dave, all were nicer than they looked.

"How do you take your coffee, Brad?" Dave asked.

"Umm, two milks, three sugars," I replied.

With that, Dave ran toward the doors to go place his order, leaving me alone with the three amigos.

"So, Lizzie, eh?" Bubba asked, smiling and winking at me. "How's that going?"

"Not too bad," I replied cautiously. "She's an amazing girl."

The three nodded silently, all sharing secret looks with one another.

"What? Did I say something wrong?"

Again, they shared a look with one another.

"Well," Sideshow said finally, tossing his finished butt to the ground and stepping on it. "Let's just say old Black Ice is gettin' soft."

I was about to say something, when something else took my attention.

"Wait…Black ice?"

The three smiled and nodded.

"Why do you call him Black Ice?" I asked.

"Should've known him back in the day, kid," Sideshow said, lighting up another stick. "He was just like black ice. Don't see it in front of you or feel it until you're right on top of it. Davey boy was just like that. A killer."

"Mr. Legault?" I asked doubtfully. 'No way."

"Trust us, kid," Buck spoke up, scratching his beard. "Black Ice was a walking, talking hazard on the road."

They began entertaining me with horror stories about the man formerly known as Black Ice, each one graphic and terrible.

"One time, when Lizzie was little he bought her a puppy," Sideshow told. "One day the pup got into the neighbour's yard, took a crap right on the guy's lawn while he read the morning paper. The guy got up, grabbed the pup, and kicked it over the fence while little Lizzie watched."

"You're kidding."

"Nope," he continued. "Anyway, Dave got home from work and Linda was still comforting Liz. The pup was alright, but Dave, wow, he got good and mad. Went next door, grabbed Mr. Neighbour by the legs, got into the car, drove off with the driver door open and dragged the guy two blocks while holding on to his ankles."

I stared, open mouthed. They were all grinning; pleased with the trauma they were feeding me.

"Yeah, ole' Black Ice ain't as slick as he used to be," Buck said, shaking his head.

"Why's that?" I asked. "What happened?"

"Old age happened, kid," Sideshow replied. "Family and settlin' down kind of took over."

"A man don't stop ridin because he's getting old, jackass," Bubba said, flexing his aging muscles. "It's when a man stops ridin that he's old."

They all nodded in unison, each one coming to some wise biker boy agreement.

"Still," Bubba continued, "You don't poke a Kodiak just because he's hibernating."

"Telling the kid about the old days, I see."

Dave walked back into the circle and handed me my coffee.

"Thank you," I said. "So…were you guys part of a gang?"

All of them exchanged an amused look, before stretching their arms straight out in front of them, revealing an identical tattoo on each of their forearms: a red, clawed hand wrapped tightly around a flaming skull.

"Cool," I said, smiling. "What is it?"

"It's our emblem," Dave said, irritated. "back in the day we were known as the Ussher Street Devils."

"Who came up with the name?" I asked.

"I did," Dave replied. "It was the name of the street most of us grew up on. That's how most of us met."

"Sort of sounds like you originally wanted to be the next big boy band," I quipped.

They laughed as Dave pretended to send a fist into my face.

I flinched.

They laughed some more.

And the afternoon went on like that, as these middle-aged Mad Max wannabes chatted about the open road and what it was like to wear assless chaps.

I may have made the second part up, but I could have sworn Bubba mentioned them.

"So I heard some of the old crew is riding into town this week," Sideshow said suddenly, taking a final sip of his coffee. "What you think Ice? Reunion ride?"

"No shit?" Dave asked. "That'd be great to go for another ride with all the guys again."

He frowned, looking up at the sky.

"It's supposed to storm this weekend, though."

"So what?" Buck remarked, an unlit cigarette between his teeth. "Best way to watch a storm is from the mirrors over your handlebars."

Dave smiled, his answer obvious.

"I'm in."

With that, we all commenced our 'goodbyes' and 'nice to meet you's.'

As Dave and I stood and watched, the three others strapped on their gear, each one containing messages like *Bite Me!*, *I'm not good with names, mind if I call you shithead?* and *Smile! It's the second best thing you can do with your lips* plastered all over their helmets.

With a kick and a final wave, all three rode off into the afternoon sun.

With a nod and a shrug, Dave and I got into the car and made our way home.

* * *

That night, after a mouth-watering supper of homemade fettuccine alfredo, the four of us made a few drinks, grabbed a few lawn chairs and watched the fireworks hit the sky from their back yard.

A couple hours later, when Elizabeth's eyelids began to droop, we decided to call it a night and head in.

After saying goodnight and thank you a dozen times for their hospitality the entire week, I headed down to the guestroom to get ready for bed.

After a quick tooth cleaning and face wash, I flicked off the bathroom light and scurried out, eagerly awaiting to dive into the soft mattress and warm, squishy sheets for the night.

But as I rounded the corner into the bedroom, I felt myself go rigid with shock.

Liz was perched on the edge of the bed, laying back on her elbows, nothing on her except an oversized T-shirt, which pulled back as she stretched out, revealing a tinge of baby blue at her waist.

"Liz," I gasped, still shocked at the sight of the goddess before me. "What are you doing?"

"Just saying goodnight," she said seductively.

"Are you crazy?" I said, teetering slightly as the feeling started to come back into my legs. "Your parents are right upstairs."

She sat up on the bed and lifted the shirt slowly above her head, revealing the beautiful bounty underneath.

"They were asleep before their heads hit the pillow," she said, smiling. "Now get over here."

I pinched myself.

No dream.

Making my way over to the bed, I quickly removed my own shirt and threw it on the floor.

No telling me twice.

Reaching the foot of the bed, I bent towards her.

She drew back, allowing her slender body to lie flat against the bed, her head inches from the pillow.

Placing my hands on the bed, I slowly crawled above her immobile form, coming to a stop right above her, our faces inches from one another.

"You've been really amazing this whole week," she said softly, looking deep into my eyes. "I don't even know where to start with what a wonderful guy you are."

"It's nothing," I said back. "I had a great time, your family's really something."

We stared at one another, each one of us too caught up in the moment to make the first move.

"Are you sure about this?" I asked soothingly, careful not to let her hear any anxiousness in my voice.

"Kiss me," the temptress said.

And, locked tightly in a passionate embrace, we made love.

* * *

The next morning Liz and her mom rose early to run a few errands before the two us headed back to school.

Dave was out back cutting the grass. I had just woke up, still a little light-headed from the events of the past night.

After a piece of toast and a cup of coffee, I went back to my room and packed up my bags.

As I started loading them into my car, I felt a buzzing coming from my jeans' pocket.

Reaching in, I pulled out my cell phone, and hit the Call button.

"Hello?"

"B-Rad! It's Tim!"

"Timbo! What's going on chief?"

"Not much, bro. You still with Legault?"

"Yeah. She's out with her mom right now. I'm just packing up the car."

"You gonna be back this afternoon?"

"Should be. But I'm bringing the car back to my dad's soon as I drop Liz off."

"Liz? You got pet names for each other already?"

"Ha-Ha. Got one for you too, dickhead."

"Nice. So was the week torture or what?"

"No, actually. Hell of a lot better than I expected."

"Oh yeah?"

"Yeah, man. Her parents are pretty cool. The dad's a badass. Guy's covered in tattoos, rides a Harley, used to tear up roads and people with his old biker gang."

"Oh man, listen to you!"

"What are you talking about?"

"Dude, you're starting to sound like a relationship guy. Taking a trip, meeting her parents, bragging about her dad. I thought you just went so you could get laid?"

I looked up quickly, scanning the area around me and the car I was standing next to.

No one was around. The sound of a lawnmower was still buzzing angrily from behind the house.

Sandwiching the phone between my ear and my shoulder, I opened the car trunk and started loading the bags in.

"I did, you jackass. And mission accomplished, by the way."

"No joke? My Bradley became a man?"

"Yup. Twice. All within an hour."

"Dude! You're a gunslinger, locked and loaded!"

"I should write a book, eh?"

"So now what? You going to suggest marriage to her when you get back?"

"The only suggestion I plan on making is for her to keep the tears from falling on my dad's dashboard. He'll freak and I can't afford to pay for her blubbering."

"You're not even going to wait until you're back to tell her? That's cold, dude."

"The sooner she hears it the better. No need to hold it off, right?"

"What if she loves you kimosabe? You sure you can do it?"

"It's college, Tim. If love exists, it's only for thirty or less in the bedroom, am I right?"

"So you really nailed her, eh?"

I laughed into the phone.

"I'll send you the video. You be the judge."

The bags loaded, I grabbed the phone, straightened up and slammed the lid of the trunk down.

Standing at the foot of the car was Dave.

I froze, caught in the headlights of his eyes, neither one of us moving.

My insides squirmed like they were alive and on fire, each one a worm, climbing over the next to escape.

He just stood there, arms folded, fixing me with a stare I had never seen before.

It was as if the nickname had come to show itself, and a blindfold was lifted over my eyes.

I hadn't seen it coming. I had been moving too casually, speeding along, too cocky and sure of myself to slow down.

And now, fixed in his stare, I felt myself careening wildly, the next victim to Black Ice's hidden menace.

"So," he said, his voice quiet but full of restrained venom.

The sound of a lawn mower interrupted my panic, as the sound of its motor came closer.

Suddenly, to my left, the next door neighbour appeared from the side of the house, unaware of the two of us locked in a faceoff as he began to cut his front lawn.

"Mr. Legault," I stammered, stuffing the phone back into my pocket. "I can explain..."

Raising his hand in the air, he cut me off before I could say anything else.

"Five minutes," he finally said.

The connection with what he was saying hit me instantly. I slowly made my way to the driver's side door, both eyes still locked on Dave.

When I reached the car door, I grasped the latch and pulled.

Dave unfolded his arms and started backing up towards the screen door of the house.

"Five minutes," he repeated. "Make them count."

And with that he turned around and stormed inside.

I jumped into the car and shut the door.

I sat there, gripping the wheel, drenched in a cold sweat, my mind racing.

"Shit!" I yelled to no one, slamming my hands against the wheels. "Shit! Shit! Shit!"

Suddenly a humming noise entered my ears.

Horrified, I looked through the windshield.

The garage door was beginning to rise.

Panicking, I threw the key into the ignition and started the car.

Looking up, I saw movement coming from the shadows of the garage interior.

A roar, loud, deafening and vicious, filled the air.

Black Ice was about to ride out on the back of his dragon.

Breaking out of my trance, I kicked my pony into reverse and backed up onto the street.

Switching gears, I hit the gas for all she was worth and took off.

* * *

I had been driving for twenty minutes when I saw it:

The gas light was on.

"Damn you!" I shouted at the car.

I was mere minutes from the Interstate, but I needed gas now.

Ahead and to the right, I saw a service station.

Making up my mind, I looked into every mirror, once, twice, three times.

No sign of him.

Turning on my indicator, I pulled into the station and lined up with one of the pumps.

Getting out, I quickly made my way around the side of the car, screwed off the gas cap and grabbed a pump.

Flipping the switch down, I inserted the pump into the car and squeezed the handle.

And then I heard it.

Low at first, like a bee or a mosquito that flies too close to your ear.

And then the buzz became a growl, louder, deeper and more frightening.

Looking back the way I came I saw him.

It was Dave.

No, wait.

It was Dave…and Bubba…and Sideshow…and Buck.

And a hell of a lot more.

The Ussher Street Devils were riding again.

With a quick glance from behind the tinted aviators bridged on his nose, Dave raised his left arm up and down with his index finger pointed to the skies.

Without even understanding how, I knew what it meant.

He was telling them to speed up.

Letting go of the pump's trigger, I threw it to the side, quickly screwed the cap back on and ran to the car door.

The station attendant came running out as I started my car.

Giving him the finger, I hit the gas and sped off.

Checking my mirror, I got a closer look at the monsters gaining on me.

Dave was in the lead, his face set in his mission.

Extermination.

I shook my head, telling my brain to focus on my own mission.

Avoiding extermination.

It was a beautiful sunny day. The sun was burning madly above us, and I flipped the visor down to get it out of my eyes.

Speeding up as I got on to the interstate, I caught a glint coming from my left. I looked into the side mirror.

The sun, infuriated with my visor flip, had seemingly focused all of its strength and radiance on to another object:

The chrome of Dave's bike.

It bounced off of every glistening, gleaming piece of chrome on the roaring beast, and that's when I remembered something Dave had told me.

"...there ain't nothing prettier in this world than sunshine on chrome."

Funny how one man's vision of beauty becomes another's moment of fear isn't it?

I looked back down at the gas gauge.

I had barely made a dent, watching as the gauge slowly quivered back towards empty.

I'm running out of gas.

I just hope they run out first.

# A Sonnet For Jennifer

*By Chris*

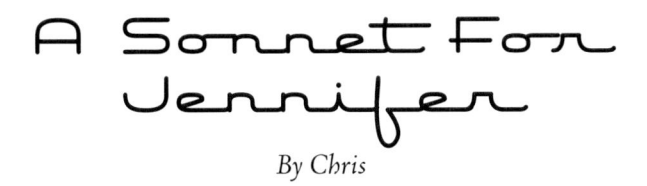

How beautiful a life we've made as two
Love is a lock and we are the two keys
Struggles and hardships we've pushed our way through
Times gone by become distant memories

Things we have done and the time we have spent
Our life together is one meant to be
Words of love spoken were truthfully meant
I look in your eyes and true love I see

I look ahead at our years yet to come
I wonder what joys tomorrow will bring
When I'm without you I'm deaf, blind and dumb
When we're together you make my heart sing

I love you with all I am and will be
I want you and need you here next to me

# Cindy

*By Chris*

Life for her had been wonderful right up until the time Brandon had been born. Being a sick baby like he was, she had become nothing but invisible to her parents for the first month of his life.

Their time was mostly divided between the hospital and sleep. She had spent most of that month in the company of strangers. Her parents leaving her with anyone and everyone they could while they tended to her newborn brother.

She didn't mind though. She was happy to have a little brother. At thirteen, she was now no longer an only child.

Her parents had finally agreed after a month of begging to let her go with them to the hospital one evening. They cautioned her on the drive that what she was going to see was not a pretty sight.

When thay got to the hospital, they had taken her up to the Intensive Care Unit. After donning gowns and masks, they walked over to the pediatrics viewing area. What she saw through the window broke her heart.

Brandon was no bigger than her two palms put together. She had known that being premature he would be small, but this was more than just small. This was tiny.

He was on his back, arms and legs splayed out to the sides. His diaper was the smallest she had ever seen, like something you would put on a doll, but even it looked like it would just fall right off if you dared to pick him up.

Tubes ran from his mouth, nose, and even from his diaper. The tubes, although very small were still thicker than his little fingers.

She watched as his tiny belly rose and fell with each breath. Her eyes welled up and soon tears flowed down her face. She reached up and placed her hand on the glass. It was as if she was trying to give him something through the glass. Energy, nourishment, life. She felt helpless.

She looked over at her parents, who had moved away and were now talking to one of the doctors. The doctor had a folder open and was showing her parents something inside.

She looked back at the baby and was surprised to see that his head was now turned in her direction. His eyes were open just a sliver. Even though there was medication oozing out from under the lids, she still felt like he was looking at her.

His tiny arm raised up, almost seemed to be reaching out to her. She put her hand back up to the glass.

His hand fell.

Machines started beeping.

Nurses and doctors ran into the room.

Her mother was screaming.

Her father was holding his mother.

The doctor in the room was holding something.

She heard the doctor yell, "CLEAR!"

\* \* \*

It was a tough time after the funeral. Her mother was either asleep or so doped up on the pills the doctors were feeding her, that she had lost her job. Because of this, her father had to get a second job just to support the family. When her father was home, he was either sleeping or drunk. Everyone was dealing in their own way.

One day she had come home from school and her mother was gone. She had gone into the bedroom to check on her, and found a note her mother had left for her father. What it amounted to was that she couldn't bear to be around anymore, because seeing him and Cindy only reminded her of losing Brandon.

\* \* \*

Her father drank even more after that. One day she came home from school and found him sitting at the kitchen table. There was a mostly empty bottle of booze in front of him.

"No work today Daddy?" She asked as pleasantly as she could.

He mumbled something about being fired, and then poured the rest of the bottle into his glass. She grabbed a snack, walked over, kissed him on the cheek, then hurriedly retreated to her room. She wasn't afraid of him, not exactly, but there was something about his demeanor when he was drinking that made her uncomfortable.

Here she was safe. This was her space, her haven.

Ever since the death of her brother, when she wasn't at school, she was in her room. Whether it was to get away from her drunken father, her doped up mother, or just to write in her journals, she spent almost all of her waking hours here.

She was now almost living her life like a hermit, other than school, she had no interaction with other kids her age. While the other thirteen year olds were on their phones gossiping about boys or each other, she was here, staring at the walls, or writing her thoughts down in tight, neat script.

* * *

It was a few days later that she came home to find her father once again drunk, but this time he wasn't at the table, he was sitting on the edge of her bed. He had one of her journals in his hand while the others were scattered about the room. As she stood in the doorway, he looked up from his reading.

"This is all my fault?" He asked her.

"What are you talking about Daddy?" She asked as she dropped her schoolbag and began to pick up her journals.

He scanned the page for a second. "Daddy is drinking more now. I wish he would stop so that things can go back to normal." He said in a mock girls voice.

"But I…" She began.

"It's my fault your mother left?" He asked as he got to his feet.

"That's not…"

"It's my fault your brother died?"

"I didn't…."

His hand cut her words off before she could get them out. She fell to the ground, her face stinging, and tears rolling down her cheeks. She pulled herself into the corner. Pulling her knees up to her chest, she sat there looking at him looming over her.

She saw as his eyes began to well up. He opened his mouth to speak but no words came out. He reached out his hands to her, and she buried her head in her knees. After a moment she raised her head up and he was gone. She sat for a moment longer then slowly got to her feet. She walked over to the mirror on her dresser.

Her face was swollen where he had struck her, and she could see a perfect red handprint had formed. The tears had stopped, and she set about cleaning up her room.

* * *

The teachers asked about her black eye the next day, to which she gave the ages old excuse that she had walked into a door. Most of the teachers brushed it off, but one teacher, Mrs. Camarillo. She wouldn't let it slide. After finally convincing her it was nothing, Cindy was able to go through the rest of her day relatively unnoticed.

Near the end of the day she was called down to the Guidance Councillor's office.

She sat in one of the chairs outside the door and waited. After what seemed like an eternity but was really only five minutes, the Guidance Councillor, Ms. Coy opened the door and poked her head out.

"Cindy." She said, "Come on in sweetie."

She got up from her chair and trudged into the room. Ms. Coy closed the door behind them and motioned for Cindy to sit in a chair in front of her desk. Cindy sat and waited as Ms. Coy walked to the other side and sat. Ms. Coy sat up and looked at her.

"How are you Cindy?" She asked.

"I'm fine." Cindy replied.

"How are you finding school this year?"

"It's fine."

"Have you made new friends this year?"

"Not really."

They sat silently for a second. Before Ms. Coy could ask another question, Cindy spoke.

"A door." She said.

"What's that sweetie?" Ms. Coy asked.

"I walked into a door." Cindy said. "Isn't this why I'm here?" She questioned as she pulled the hair back from her face and pointed to her eye.

"Actually yes it is." Ms. Coy stated.

They talked for a few more minutes. Ms. Coy trying hard to get Cindy to give up something, anything that would lead her to believe that it wasn't really a door, but Cindy held firm to her story.

Cindy left Ms. Coy's office and on her way back to class, stopped in the girl's room. As she was sitting in the stall, she heard a couple of other girls come in. She listened for a second to see who it was. It was Sabrina and Kristy. Two friends from her class. She was about to get out of the stall when she heard something that made her stop.

"Ms. Coy told Mrs. Camarillo that if she finds out it was her dad, then they are going to take her away." Sabrina said.

"Can you imagine?" Kristy asked.

"What?" Sabrina questioned.

"First, her baby brother dies, then her mother leaves, now her father starts beating her."

"Wow, I never thought of all that." Sabrina said.

The two girls finished their business in silence. Assumedly brooding over Cindy's dramatic life. After a minute the two of them left.

Cindy continued to sit for a while after they were gone. She finally got up, washed away the tear streaks from her face, washed her hands, and was going to make her way back to class when a feeling overwhelmed her and she ran down the hall, straight out the front doors.

* * *

She ran down the front steps.

She ran down the street.

She ran until a stitch in her side forced her to slow and walk.

Not knowing how far she had come, she took a moment to look around. She was in a park now. She had run from the sidewalk onto the footpath leading through it. After a moment she realized where she was.

The park was six blocks from her school. The opposite direction of her home. Had she run the opposite way on purpose? She wasn't sure. The run had tired her, her emotions had tired her. She walked slowly, her hand pressed to her side, trying to ease the pain of the cramp. When she finally came to an empty bench, she sat.

As she sat she could feel something building up inside of her. Suddenly the dam burst and her emotions came flooding out fast and furious. Everything she had been holding inside for the last few months came out at once.

She cried.

She cried harder than she had ever cried before. She cried for the baby brother she never got to know. She cried for the mother she knew and loved, but lost. She cried for the father who once adored her. She used to be "Daddy's little girl", she used to feel special. Now she just felt in the way.

"Excuse me."

Thoughts raced through her mind at a frenzied pace. Should she go home? Would it be better if she ran away?

"Excuse me."

She didn't know what to do. If she ran, where would she go? She couldn't go to a relative's house. They would just call her father.

She jumped when she felt the hand come to rest on her shoulder. She looked and saw an old man looking down at her. "Excuse me." He said.

She was surprised.

"Are you all right?" The old man asked.

"I..I'm fine." Cindy replied, wiping the tears from her face.

"Are you sure? You look like you're in some kind of trouble."

She looked the old man over. He was short and very thin. He was holding a cane in one hand so she assumed he had trouble walking. He looked like a strong wind would actually knock him over. She looked at his face. It seemed kind. Especially his eyes. When she looked into his eyes, she felt no threat whatsoever. Only kindness seemed to reside there.

"I'm not in trouble." She replied to him.

"Did someone hurt you?" He asked as he sat down on the other end of the bench.

Before she knew what had happened, she found she had told him the entire story. He listened patiently, without question or interruption, allowing her to get it all out.

"Quite sad." He said.

"I just don't know what to do." She said as fresh tears stung the corners of her eyes.

"I can't tell you what you should do, little lady, the decision is your and yours alone."

When he stopped talking, she looked at him. "What would you do?" She asked.

He looked over and began.

"Your story is not exactly unique." He began. "At some point in almost everyone's life they will suffer through pain and loss, and it is up to each individual to find their own way through it."

"Did you lose someone?" Cindy asked.

He looked at her and she could see his face soften even more as he continued.

"I lost my son. Many years ago now." He said.

"What happened to him?"

"There were some men," he started, "who thought my son deserved to die because of some things he was saying and doing."

The old man stopped, tilted his head back and closed his eyes.

"My son died a horrible death." He continued. "But it was through his death that those men were proven wrong, and many others were saved."

"Do you have other kids?" Cindy asked.

"I have many children." The old man replied.

"Did you treat them differently after that?"

He thought for a moment. "Even though sometimes my children feel like I am not there for them, or they feel like I am ignoring them, or they feel like I do things to make them suffer, I have never stopped loving them."

"Do they know you love them, no matter what?" Cindy asked.

"Some of them do. Some don't realize how much they are loved."

"I wish my Daddy still loved me like that." She said softly, looking down at her hands resting in her lap.

"Oh he does, Cindy, he does."

"How do you know that?

"If he didn't love you, he wouldn't be out looking for you." He replied.

"Why would he be looking for me, it's not lat…" She cut her own words off as she looked around and realized night had fallen.

Confused, she stood up and took two steps away from the bench. "How is it so late?" She asked.

When no answer came, she looked at the bench but the old man was gone.

"*CINDY!*" Someone called in the distance.

She went to the bench and sat back down.

"*CINDY!*" The voice called, closer now. She looked and could see a light bobbing along the path.

She looked at the other end of the bench. Where did he go? Was he ever really there?

"*CINDY!*" The voice exclaimed as the bobbing light focused on her. It was her father.

She stood as the light bobbed faster now. She could hear his footfalls as he ran to her. In turn she ran toward him. They ran into each others arms and both of them held on tightly.

"I'm so sorry." Her father sobbed. "I'm so sorry sweetheart."

"Me too Daddy." She said as fresh tears once again flowed.

"I was so worried, baby." He held her at arms length and she could see tears streaming down his face as well. He pulled her back and held her tight again. "I'm sorry sweetie. I love you baby."

"I love you too Daddy."

\* \* \*

Her father sold the house shortly after. He had stopped drinking, found a new job, and was spending as much time with Cindy as he could.

They moved to an apartment on the other side of town. She had had to change schools but thought it was for the better anyway. In a new school no one knew her, or her past. The only thing they could judge her on was the fact that she was new. They had nothing on her. She used to walk shyly, with her head down.

She now walked with confidence.

She now walked with strength.

She now walked with faith.

# The Litttle Things

*By Tom*

*A fresh cup of Joe would really hit the spot right now*, he thought.

Two creams.

Two sugars.

Sweet perfection.

He sat there, perched upon a log that was adorned with a layer of dampened moss, head in his hands, entranced by the beauty around him.

He had been sitting there for hours. No cell phone. No portable radio. No noise.

Just the sounds of the wilderness around him. Alone with nothing but his thoughts and Mother Nature.

He had forgotten how perfect a sunrise could be.

Forgotten how sweet the fresh air tasted on his tongue.

He inhaled deeply, making sure to savour the taste of fresh life escaping his lips as he exhaled.

He smiled. Oh, the little things.

Breaking apart clumps of dry earth with his shoes, the man inattentively created a perfect circle in the dirt, apparently lost in the recess of his own thoughts.

Two squirrels caught his eye as they came scurrying by, one in pursuit of the other. He watched them, transfixed, as they ran up the bark of a tree into the arms of the branches and leaves above, and out of sight.

It was at that moment, that the unfortunate reality of the situation forced its way through the serenity of his mind.

What now?

He was strapped for cash. No food. No car.

Thousands of miles from home sweet home and a long, hot shower.

Sighing heavily, he rose to his feet, brushing away any traces of dirt or leaves from his clothes.

*There's no use sitting here till sunset*, he thought. *Plan or no plan, I gotta keep moving.*

Zipping up his jacket, he started walking; silently hoping wherever he was going led to a busy road and at least one Good Samaritan.

* * *

"I'm so sick of driving", the man said aloud.

Two days, he thought.

Two days stuck behind this godforsaken wheel, only getting out to fill up on gas or to take a leak.

He looked around.

Nothing but highway road, trees and…well, that was about it.

The song on the radio ended, and he quickly turned up the volume as the news came on.

After a couple minutes of attentive listening, he turned the volume back down, a disgusted look on his face.

Nothing but weather reports and celebrity gossip.

Nothing important.

He squinted through the windshield glass, as sleep's soothing call beckoned to him.

Caffeine, he thought, rubbing his eyes. He needed caffeine.

Ignoring the hours old coffee sitting half empty in its holder, the driver decided he would get a fresh one at the next exit.

Something further down the road suddenly caught his attention.

It was a man.

He was still too far away to distinguish any of the man's features, but he could see what the man was doing.

He was standing, motionless, at the edge of the road.

Outstretched arm.

Closed fist.

Thumb in the air.

A hitchhiker.

Backpacker.

Wayfarer, if you will.

He didn't have a problem with hitchhikers.

He knew a lot of people did, however.

Whether out of cautious fear or just a plain lack of concern, most peopled tended to speed up and look straight ahead once they saw a thumb in the air.

But the driver didn't share the same feelings.

In fact, he had provided transportation on more than one occasion for those stranded souls and the worst that had come out of it for him were some awkward silences brought on by a lack of conversation or a foreign language.

Before he knew it, he had already turned on his truck's indicator light and was slowly making his way to the shoulder of the road.

He came to a stop about 10 feet from where the hitcher stood, so as to get a good look at the man's appearance.

He looked to be in his 30's, the driver observed.

He was average height, with a slim build and pale complexion.

He had a square face, topped with a short but slicked back haircut, and centred with a slightly crooked nose, which the driver assumed to be the result of one too many run-ins with a hard object.

There was a bit of a sunken look in the man's face that was partially covered by the shadows of a beard.

It was the way the way this man was dressed, however, that caught the driver's attention.

His attire was normal enough; casual clothes from a chequered button-up shirt, a beige suede jacket, to a pair of faded jeans.

But something wasn't right with it.

Or rather, the driver noticed, something didn't quite fit.

The jeans clung a little too snug to his skin, and the bottoms were barely down to his ankles.

The suede jacket hung loosely enough, but perhaps the man's arms weren't proportionate to the rest of his body, because the sleeves didn't go all the way to his wrist, which exposed the bare skin and noticeable tattoos going up each arm.

"Afternoon!" the driver called to the man, nodding to the passenger door.

The hitcher seemed rooted to the spot, a look of seemingly complete astonishment still etched upon his face, as though shocked someone had just stopped and acknowledged him.

After a few seconds the man seemed to get his bearings, and slowly made his way over to the truck.

"Afternoon", he finally replied, staring at the driver with slight curiosity. "How goes it?"

The driver smiled.

"It goes. Lost your way?"

The hitcher stared back at him.

"You could say that."

The driver looked out down the stretch of highway road.

"Where you headed?" he asked.

The hitchhiker followed his gaze, but took a few seconds to respond.

"It's a long story, but…I haven't exactly figured that out yet," he finally said.

The driver nodded, drumming his fingers off the top of the steering wheel.

"I see," he said. "Well, I've got about a four-day drive on the go and two days down already. Think you could find yourself a destination in between here and where I'm headed?"

The wayfarer looked completely taken aback by the question.

"Wait," he said, a look of disbelief on his face. "You're offering me a ride?"

The driver smiled again.

"Wasn't that what you were hoping for?"

"Well…yeah," the hitchhiker replied, confusion in his eyes. "But you don't exactly know anything about me, and you're just going to let me into your car?"

"Good point," the driver replied, scratching his chin. "Alright then. What's your name?"

The hitchhiker looked stunned.

"Ch…Chase," he replied.

"Well Chase," the driver said, extending his hand to the passenger window. "I'm Mike. And I am offering you transportation to wherever it is you decide to call home. Fair enough?"

Chase stood motionless for a few seconds, before grinning and shaking the man's hand.

"You sure I'm not a serial killer or something?" he asked.

Mike laughed and leaned back against his seat.

"I like to consider myself a pretty good judge of character. And to be honest, I don't see myself in any type of mortal peril by doing this. Door's unlocked, Chase."

The grin never fading from his face, Chase opened the door, sat himself down in the vinyl seat, and buckled himself in.

"I forgot to mention," Mike said suddenly, looking serious. "There's just one…let's say, condition to you hitching a ride with me."

Chase jolted up in surprise.

"Oh?" he asked, hesitantly.

Mike looked sideways to face him and stared directly into his eyes.

"First," he replied, putting the gear into Drive. "We get coffee."

Chase exhaled quickly, feeling somehow relieved at the answer.

"That," he said eagerly, "sounds perfect."

\* \* \*

Chase counted himself a lucky man.

He had not counted on things working so well for him, and Mike stopping at the side of the road had been the biggest stroke of luck so far.

He had not asked Chase for money. A favour. Not a single thing.

*And thank God for that*, Chase thought. *I don't have two cents on me.*

No, Mike seemed to be one of those few people who simply sympathized with his situation.

"I really do appreciate this," Chase said, breaking the silence that had begun to creep up between them. "There aren't too many Good Samaritans left out there."

"It's not a problem," Mike replied, eyes still on the road. "I'd like to think somebody would do the same for me, if the situation were reversed."

Chase nodded, looking back out the window.

The scenery was less than interesting.

Trees.

A patch of open field.

A lone cow if he was lucky.

More trees.

"So where did you say you were hea…," Chase started.

"Hold on!" Mike interrupted suddenly, turning up the dials on the radio. "The news!"

Chase quickly went quiet, already used to Mike's random infatuation with the hourly news updates.

*It had been the only unusual thing about the guy*, Chase thought.

If you could call that unusual.

Although he had been sitting down through their entire meeting thus far, Mike appeared to be a reasonably well-built man, probably in his late 30s, early 40s.

He had a heart-shaped face, topped with brown, surfer-boy hair that went down just past his ears.

He was a good-looking guy, but definitely looked like he had been behind the wheel for a few days.

There were dark marks under his almond-shaped, blue-green eyes, and he had a few days of growth on his cheeks and neck.

The heavy, black leather jacket Mike had been wearing was now draped over the back of his seat, revealing the white, long-sleeved thermal shirt underneath.

A reporter's voice rang over the radio:

"*In recent news, the Blue Odyssey, a cruise ship in the coast of Mexico, is now dead in the water after a fire broke out in the ship's engine room.*

*Reports say no one was injured in the fire, but the main generators of the ship have been disabled, leaving operations such as climate, sewage disposal and other functions without power.*

*Helicopters are now flying in hot me…*"

Chase lost interest quickly, and resorted to once again scanning the interior of the truck out of boredom.

A complete mess, he thought. That was the only way to describe it.

Clothes were carelessly left unfolded and heavily wrinkled in the tiny back seats, spotted with grease and coffee stains from the discarded coffee cups and burger wrappers keeping them company.

His eyes moved to the front.

The glove compartment was swelling with the desire to burst, the countless maps and guides aching to break out.

A tiny wooden crucifix hung from the rear-view mirror, the letters AZRAEL carved neatly into the wood in a vertical line.

"Azrael?" Chase said, louder than he thought.

"Childhood nickname," Mike replied, his focus clearly not on the question.

*Ok then*, Chase thought, getting the point, his attention drifting back to the view outside.

*Or lack thereof*, he thought miserably, noticing the increase of trees and forest on either side of them.

He looked up and noticed the sun was making its descent, casting a pink-orange glow over the darkening skies.

"*...today also marks 15 years since the first murder by the killer known as the Grim Reaper. The Grim Reaper has been responsible for at least 30 murders throughout North America, his last one occurring in January more than two years ago...*"

"I've heard of that guy!" Chase yelled, his attention snapping back to the radio.

"Have you?" Mike replied, a smile evident on his face. "You and the rest of the world."

"Shut it," Chase retorted, now smiling. "I'm just saying. He's been a topic of conversation before."

"Oh?" Mike said, turning down the radio. "Do tell."

Chase straightened up in his seat, carefully going over the words in his head.

"My old roommates and I used to talk about him a couple years back," he said.

"Apparently the guy never killed in the same place twice. And every victim the cops found was the same: eyes open and head shaved, save for a single lock of hair."

Mike stole a quick glance over him.

"Why'd he leave a lock of hair?" he asked.

"One of my roomies said it was given as a token to the Devil so that one day the Reaper could return to the Underworld," Chase shrugged.

Mike shuddered slightly.

"Not the most pleasant road trip conversation," he murmured.

"That's not even the worst of it."

"Oh?" Mike asked tentatively.

"Yeah," Chase replied. "The cops had a hell of a time figuring out what weapon the killer was using, cuz' every body was a bloody mess."

"They never found out what it was?" Mike asked.

"Oh they found out," Chase replied. "Doin' all that CSI crap they do, they figured out it was a scythe."

"A scythe?" Mike inquired.

"Yeah. One of those olden day hand tools farmers used for reaping crops. Long blade,…"

"Ok, I think I've heard enough," Mike declared.

"Hey, you asked," Chase said in defence.

"True enough," Mike said. "Wish I hadn't now."

"Scared?" Chase asked, grinning.

"No," Mike replied, unconvincingly, his mouth twitching.

"Hey, I get it," Chase said. "It's makes complete sense why that would scare you."

Mike glanced over at him, a doubtful look stretching his features.

"Oh?" he said.

Chase avoided his gaze.

"Sure," he said seriously. "A pretty boy like you, parting with that mane? My God, what would you do?"

Mike rolled his eyes, as his passenger laughed quietly at his own joke.

* * *

The two spent the next couple hours debating possibilities of Chase's future living arrangements.

Outside, night had fallen, the moon taking its place among surrounding stars.

"So you have no living family?" Mike asked. "No one that you can stay with?"

Chase shifted uncomfortably in his seat.

"Nope. Parents died a long time ago. Never been married. Never had kids."

"No siblings?"

"Just a younger brother," Chase replied.

"And where is he?" Mike asked.

"Died. Couple days ago, actually."

Mikes foot slipped off the gas pedal in shock.

"Chase…I'm so sorry. It was none of my business. I shouldn't have asked."

"No, it's ok," Chase said waving his hand in the air. "Don't apologize. It's kind of the reason I'm looking for somewhere new."

Mike nodded in understanding.

"I can appreciate that. Sometimes it's hard to continue living where pain and damage are present. Sometimes it's just easier to…escape."

Chase said nothing, but looked quietly out the window.

"It's getting late," he said, noticing the darkness and lack of cars around them. "Should we stop for the night?"

Mike rubbed his eyes, blinking them open and closed a few times.

"Good idea. I'll get off at the next exit we see."

Quiet broke out between them, as The Animals' *The House of the Rising Sun* filled the confines of the truck.

"*…And God I know I'm one…*" the song ended, and Mike turned up the volume, once again preparing for the news.

"*…And now this late-breaking news report. According to police, two nights ago brothers Charles and Douglas Jones escaped from a maximum security pri…*"

*We need to get off the road,* Chase thought, looking out the window as Mike turned on his indicator light and entered the exit lane.

"*…arrested three years ago for armed robbery and the brutal slayings of five innocent bystanders, the Jones brothers were sentenced to…*"

*C'mon,* Chase thought. *Think.*

"*Two nights ago, a bus transporting prisoners from…*"

*Think dammit, think!*

The voice on the radio continued.

"*brothers escaped, fleeing on foot, last being witnessed hijacking a car at a gas sta…*"

Chase felt a bead of sweat running slowly down his forehead towards the edge of his eyelash.

"*…both are described as 5 foot 9, slim build and adorned with tattoos spreading from hands to neck. Although these two brothers were not armed* upon exit of the bus, both men are considered extremely dangerous. Caution is extremely advised."

The news ended, and a commercial for McDonald's coffee came over the air.

Chase swallowed hard.

He felt his hands shaking, and quickly clasped them together in his lap.

He stole a glance over at Mike, tense with panic.

Mike's eyes remained on the road, his face evoking no emotion.

After a few moments of silence, Mike finally spoke.

"Interesting shoes for the great outdoors aren't they?" he enquired, noticing his passenger's soccer-style shoes.

Chase's stomach did a somersault.

*He knows.*

"Yeah well, I had no money, and had to get away with the clothes on my back, you know?" Chase said quickly.

"Oh," Mike said quietly. "Yes, I suppose so."

*The time had come*, Chase thought. *Right now.*

"Mike, can you pull over? I think I'm going to be sick."

Mike snapped his head in his passenger's direction.

"What? Sick? You sure?"

Chase nodded, holding his stomach.

"Please," he gasped. "I'm gonna be sick!"

Mike swerved sharply onto the side of the road and threw his foot down on the brakes.

Chase threw open the door and jumped out of his seat.

Within seconds, Mike could hear him heaving into the greenery around them.

"You ok?" he called to the darkness.

He received nothing but a muffled gag in response.

Briefly drumming his fingers on the steering wheel, Mike quickly made a decision and jumped out of the truck, making his way around to the sick man's side.

The figure of Chase was slumped less than 10 feet from him, on its knees, head in its hands.

"Chase?" he said softly, a chill running down his spine. "You ok?"

The figure in the grass said nothing, but an eerily calm voice spoke back.

"It wasn't my choice, you know."

Mike froze in his tracks like a deer caught in the glare of a car's headlights.

*Something's not right*, he thought.

"I'm sorry?" he coughed. "What wasn't?"

The figure in the dark raised its head.

"I had plans. My brother had more important ones."

The man in the dark rose from the earth, like a cobra before the strike.

"Family," he said bitterly, his face obstructed from view in the surrounding night. "A wife. Kids. 'The dream' he called it. 'Pathetic', I told him."

As Mike looked on, he heard the man unzipping his jacket, the zipper's descent as loud and terrifying as a gunshot.

"We already had it all," he continued. "Cars. Money. Women. Had to sell our souls to the devil to get it, but it was worth it. And then my dear brother decided he wanted it back. Wanted to take back his soul and give up his freedom. It wasn't fair."

It was our last job together, and I could see his head was clouded with pictures of fairy tales and happy endings. He was careless. Foolish. We were too slow, and the cops got the jump on us."

Mike stood, transfixed, his eyes on his feet.

"My big brother froze," the man continued. "I had no choice. I had to shoot our way out. All the years, all the jobs, never one shot fired. In one night, five people killed at my feet. The cops closed in. We were surrounded. Caught like goddamn mice, ready to serve 25 years to life in a cold, dark cell."

The man took a step towards Mike, but Mike remained rooted to the spot.

*He's too terrified to move*, the man thought, smiling. *Good. This will make it easier.*

"Two nights ago, we got a taste of freedom again," he said. "We had money buried back home, in case of an emergency. But we needed a ride to make it back. We walked for hours the first night. Came up on a gas station in some little town. Just a man behind the counter inside. We had no choice. We took food, clothes, the attendant's car, and just to be safe, I took his life."

He paused, letting the words hang in the air before continuing.

"My brother was driving. Everything seemed fine. And then guess what he said to me?"

Mike didn't respond. The man kept on.

"He told me he was out. Said he was taking his share and taking off. Starting over. Told me I had cost him everything and he was gonna save whatever he had left. I couldn't have it. My brother had changed. Again, I had no choice."

"We had to ditch the truck before the cops found us. We left it at the side of the highway, and made off on foot into the woods. I waited as long as I could. When we got far enough away from the road, I came up behind my big brother of mine, I pulled out the knife I had already used back at the gas station, and threw it into his back. He went quickly, the whole time blaming me with his eyes."

Reaching into the inner pocket of his jacket, he pulled a knife out, its blade gleaming in the moonlight, blood still stained on its tip.

"This is the knife I used," he said delicately, twirling it between the fingers of his right hand. "My brother never realized it was his own mistake that brought me to my actions. Kind of like…you never realized your mistake by stopping at the side of the road today."

The man started inching closer towards Mike, knife at waist level, blade pointing towards his new prey.

"You should have kept driving, friend," he said soothingly. "Sometimes it doesn't always pay to be a guardian angel."

As he closed in on his latest victim, Mike's voice suddenly broke the deathly silence.

"2 Corinthians 11:14."

The man stopped dead in his tracks, still smiling but looking confused.

"Come again?"

Eyes still on the ground, Mike responded.

"Even Satan disguises himself as an angel of light."

The man stood silently, completely thrown by the statement.

"I'm afraid you've lost me, chie…"

"What makes you think I'm a guardian angel?" Mike interrupted, slowly raising his head. "What if it's just...part of the plan?"

The man recoiled, almost dropping his knife in shock at the sight in front of him.

When Mike had lifted his head, the moonlight danced on his face, highlighting his features.

The kindness and understanding had evaporated from his eyes, replaced by a sheet of frigid ice.

His facial features, which had earlier expressed such trust and sympathy, had been shattered, all emotion crumbling from every corner and crevasse.

A horrific transformation had taken over Mike's body.

"What the..." the man began, his voice shaking.

Before he could even move, the hitcher felt something hard connect with the side of his head, and he collapsed into a darkness blacker and more penetrating than the night around them.

* * *

The man once known as Chase awoke to the smell of burning wood.

His head was pounding fiercely, and his eyes were still closed, playing tricks on him, as dancing lights flickered on and off through his eyelids.

Feeling as if he were deep in hallucination, he opened his eyes, and was astonished to see a roaring fire less than five feet from him.

He attempted to get up out of his sitting position, and was horribly shocked to find he could not move.

Looking to his left and right, he realized his arms were stretched to full length, ropes wrapped tightly around his wrists, each end of the ropes tied around a thick tree.

*I've become the prey*, he thought. *No.*

"Welcome back, Mr. Jones," a disembodied voice whispered from the other side of the fire.

The man's head snapped back to the fire, attempting to look through the blaze.

"Where are you?" he said weakly. "Why are you doing this?"

He felt footsteps on the other side of the flames, and when the voice spoke again, it sounded closer.

"You sound frightened, my dear friend. No more than an hour ago I believe you were prepared to do even worse to me."

"Do worse to you?" the man yelled. "Mike…please…"

"Mike is not here," the voice said grimly. "Only Death."

The words were cold and terrifying, and sent a terrible chill straight down the hitcher's spine.

"Death?" he cried, recalling the crucifix. "I don't understand…"

A shape came into view through the fire.

"Your roommates, or should I say…cellmates," it said, amused. "I'm afraid they were a little off."

The man made no noise, except for the occasional whimper.

"In biblical times," the voice continued, "it was a custom to shave the head, but leave a single lock of hair, so that the Angel of Death could pull them up to heaven. Do you know the Angel's name? Think hard."

The man, struggling with the ropes that held him, could not force his mind to focus through the panic

Suddenly, from the back of his mind, came a word. He had seen it before. Etched on a crucifix…

"Azrael," he whispered.

"Very good," the voice said. "You are ready."

"Ready?" he gasped. "Ready for what?"

Bound and helpless, the man could only watch as the Grim Reaper, a man of ghost stories all across the continent, stepped into view, the dancing flames reflecting madly in the killer's eyes.

Petrified yet transfixed, the man watched in horror as the murderer made his way around the fire, stopping directly in front of his cowering body.

Bending down, the killer reached out with his right hand, his fingers running through the strands of the man's oily hair.

"For a shave, of course," the Reaper whispered.

The hitchhiker trembled beneath his gaze.

"Please," he begged. "Have…have mercy."

"Let the words of the novelist Sir Walter Scott be of some comfort to you in these final moments," the killer said, rising slowly to his feet.

"And come he slow...," the Reaper began, reaching behind the tree his victim was bound to.

"...Or come he fast...," he continued, facing the man at his feet, brandishing the scythe tightly in his hands.

"...It is but Death who comes at last."

\* \* \*

It had been over two years since his last kill.

The feelings were all coming back to him, like a drug that's effects had begun to kick in. He had forgotten how terrifying the moonlight had glinted off the curved, razor-sharp blade.

Forgotten the rush of adrenaline pumping through his body as he moved in slowly for the kill.

Forgotten the look of complete terror etched upon his victim's face, as it begged for pity.

Raising the scythe over his head like a golfer preparing the perfect swing, The Grim Reaper savoured the moment as this fellow hunter turned prey stared pleadingly back into his eyes.

He smiled. Oh, the little things.

# Welcome To The Jungle

*By Chris*

He could barely contain his excitement on the helicopter ride in. Everything he had trained the last two years for was finally happening.

He was going to be all he could be.

He was going to do his part.

Uncle Sam wanted him, so now here he was.

His enthusiasm had not gone unnoticed by his superiors. He was quickly separated from the others, and put into extensive communications training. They wanted him deep, with one of the elite groups. He had excelled at everything they had tossed at him, and when the time came, he received his assignment.

The helicopter landed in a clearing. There was a lone soldier waiting at the edge of the clearing. He hopped out the side door, pulling his pack with him. The helicopter was on the move again before he took a single step forward. He watched it go for a second, still marvelling at the fact he had actually ridden in it on his way to something big.

He walked over to the soldier, but as he approached the soldier turned and began to walk.

"Am I supposed to follow you?" He called.

The soldier just waved his arm in a follow me gesture as he continued walking away.

"Guess so." He said, slinging his pack over his back.

After walking foe twenty minutes or so, the soldier in from of him stopped. He walked up along side and stopped as well.

"Whatever you do, don't fucking salute him." The soldier said.

Before he could reply, the soldier continued walking. After following for another thirty seconds or so they emerged from the trees into another clearing. This one was larger and bustling with activity. They walked over to the far side of the clearing. Everyone here seemed to be separated into four groups. They walked over to the farthest group.

Walking between the tents they came up behind a man who was silently just watching the others.

"Sir." The soldier said.

The man turned around and looked at him. "Welcome to the jungle son, what's your name?"

Feeling more than a little intimidated and fighting the urge to salute he replied. "Stephen Bailey, sir."

"Steve-O huh?"

"Yes sir."

"That's enough with the sir shit."

"But I…"

Cutting him off the man said. "Listen, we are a really tight group here. I may be considered leader on paper, but we try really hard to remain as equals here in the G.A.A."

"G.A.A. si.." Cutting himself off, Steve started again. "G.A.A?"

"God's Arch Angels."

"God's Arch Angels." Stephen whispered to himself. "I like that."

"Yeah, we're out here cleaning up all the shit, so He doesn't have to." He said pointing upwards. "You can call me Mudsnake."

"Mudsnake?" Steve questioned.

"Yes, problem?"

"Not at all."

Pointing to the other soldier who had been silently standing there waiting, Mudsnake said, "You've already met Blue."

"Well, sort of." Smiled Steve.

"Blue is the best fucking medic out there. You should make friends with him." Mudsnake smiled. "Because if Blue wants you to live, you will."

With that statement, Blue walked away.

"I'll take you around to meet everyone else." Musnake said as he began to walk.

They emerged from between the tents, turned right and walked past the last one. On the other side of the tent was a makeshift shower. They walked over. "It draws water from a stream nearby." Musnake said. "Pretty complicated process actually."

"Really?" Steve asked.

"Yeah, when you want a shower, you take a bucket, fill it up, bring it back, and dump it into the tank up there." Mudsnake laughed.

Steve laughed as well. As they got closer he noticed it was a woman in the shower.

"Hey Juggs," Mudsnake called. "Meet the new guy, Steve-O."

"Why do you call her.." Steve stopped when she opened the curtain to shake his hand. She was covering up with one arm and shaking hands with the other but Steve could still see the reason she was called that, he felt himself blushing as they shook hands. She laughed and closed the curtain back up.

Looking at Steve, Mudsnake said, "You gotta lighten up if you're gonna fit in around here." He laughed. "Come with me."

They walked a little.

"I noticed she had some scars on her body." Steve said.

"I told you Blue was good." Mudsnake said. "She's been shot nine times and he's fixed her up everytime. Around here we call her the bulletcatcher. I personally think she's just too tough of a bitch to die."

They walked until they came to a man sitting at a small table studying a map. "This is Hall." Steve reached out and shook hands with him.

"Listen Mudsnake, I got an idea for tomorrow." Hall said.

"All right, give me a few minutes and I'll be back to go over it." Musnake replied to Hall.

Steve and Mudsnake walked away. "Hall is a very good tactician, and his advice is invaluable." Mudsnake explained.

They walked some more and Mudsnake explained the mission they were on. There was an uprising being led by a dictator. "Like a Hitler Junior," was the way Mudsnake described him. They had two communications centers set up to coordinate the uprising. Their job was to disrupt and destroy the comm centers.

Sitting under a tree were five others. They walked over and Mudsnake made the introductions. Pointing them out one at a time, Mudsnake introduced them.

"This old dude over here is Zingo." He started. "The three younger ones over there are Fuzzy, Buggy and PDX." Steve waved at each in turn. "And lastly we have Onion", Mudsnake said pointing to a woman. "Everyone, this is Steve-O."

A chorus of voices erupted from the five all at once. "STEVE-O."

All seven people burst out laughing. After a moment Mudsnake said. "I gotta go talk to Hall, hang out and get to know everyone."

Steve sat down with everyone and made small talk for a while. After a moment he turned to Onion. "Where did the name Onion come from?" He asked.

"It used to be Onionbutt, but now everyone just shortens it to Onion." she replied.

"Onionbutt?"

She stood up, turned around, and shook her butt at his face. "They called me that because my ass is so nice it makes you want to cry." She sat back down laughing.

Steve was blushing again. "It *is* nice though." he said, and with that everyone burst out laughing again.

After a while, Mudsnake and Hall came walking over. Hall went ahead and sat down.

"Steve-O, come with me," Mudsnake said.

Steve jumped to his feet and followed Mudsnake as he walked over to the tents.

"I need you to get on comms, and relay Hall's plan to the other squads."

They went inside the tent, and Steve relayed the plan step by step as Hall and Mudsnake had drawn it up. When they were finished they rejoined the others.

"Listen up," Mudsnake said. "Tomorrow is the reason we're here, so sleep tight tonight, we need everyone to be focused tomorrow."

After a few minutes of going over everyone's role the next day they all retired to their tents.

* * *

Next morning by eight o'clock they had already been trudging through the trees for two hours. Suddenly the radio Steve was carrying squawked. He got on the radio, and after a moment turned to Mudsnake.

"Everyone's in position. Waiting for your instructions." Steve told him.

"Eight Oh Five," was all Mudsnake said.

Steve relayed the message and waited. Mudsnake looked over at him.

"Nervous?" he asked.

"Not sure," Steve replied. "Excited too, I think."

"Ready to serve up some of God's justice?"

"Heck yeah."

"Heck?"

Steve smiled. "Heck." He said.

Musnake smiled back and checked his watch.

Eight Oh Four.

* * *

By eight fifty five it was over. They had dispatched the enemy with minimal casualties. Two men from the other squads had been killed, but in the G.A.A. there was only one injury. Fuzzy had been shot in the arm and was being tended to by Blue. Mudsnake and Steve walked over to check on him. Zingo was already there helping out.

"Son of a biscuit eater, that looks like it hurts." Steve said.

Blue stopped what he was doing. Fuzzy, Blue, Zingo and Mudsnake all looked at Steve.

"Biscuit eater?" asked Mudsnake.

Steve looked back. "Biscuit eater", he said matter of factly.

All five men laughed. Mudsnake clapped Steve on the shoulder and walked away shaking his head.

* * *

Later that night, Steve was approached by Zingo.

"How you holdin' up?" Zingo asked.

"I'm good." Steve replied. "You?"

"Good." Replied Zingo. "Today was a pretty easy day. Didn't have much trouble taking this comm center."

"So what now?" Asked Steve.

"We'll probably use this as a command post for a while until Mudsnake gets other orders for us."

"Is that usualy a while?"

"Nah, probably have new orders in a couple days." Zingo said. "We stay pretty busy."

"How long have you been a part of the G.A.A.?" Steve asked

"A while. It's not often we get new recruits. Mudsnake won't allow just anyone into the fold. We're like a family. Actually we are more than a family, it's not often that a family member's decisions can either cost you or save your life."

Steve thought for a moment. "Have you seen a lot of people...uh.."

"Have I seen a lot of people die?" Zingo finished for him.

"Yeah."

"Too many." Zingo said thoughtfully. "No one from the G.A.A., but other squads, yeah. And enemies? Lots."

Zingo seemed to have gone off to a faraway place in his mind so Steve didn't talk for a bit.

"What's it like?" Steve asked finally.

"What's what like?" Zingo asked back.

"To uh.. you know."

"What's it like to kill someone? It's not fun, that's for sure, if that's what you're thinking."

"Well, I wasn't exactly thinking fun, but I thought it might feel, I don't know, good." Steve replied. "Knowing you are doing the world a service. Getting rid of the bad guys."

"Is that what we're doing?" Zingo asked.

"That's what I'd like to think." Steve replied.

Zingo laughed. "As long as you keep on thinking that, son, you'll be alright. Let's go eat."

The two men left.

\* \* \*

Two months later, they were all on a plane together. Steve was now, officially a member of the G.A.A. They had been on twenty eight different missions in the last two months. Juggs had been shot again, bringing her count up to ten.

"Where we goin'?" PDX asked Mudsnake.

"Alaska." Was all Mudsnake said as he began to hand out small folders to everyone.

Everyone opened their folders as Mudsnake spoke.

"This is the big one," he started. "A militant group known as the KEQ is developing a new chemical weapon in a large facility in a remote location."

"It's a new grenade with the chemical inside." Buggy said reading ahead of everyone. "It dissipates fast, but if you are caught in the smoke before it goes it'll kill you."

"PP smoke." Said Steve quietly to himself.

Everyone laughed when suddenly the hold on the plane began to rumble open. The men and women scrambled to get their parachutes on, grab their weapons and make their way to the opening.

"This is the big one, let's do this." Mudsnake said as he jumped from the plane.

Onion followed close behind him yelling out, "Whoop whoop." The others followed in turn with Steve going out last.

As soon as his parachute deployed Steve could immediately see that something was wrong. A full scale battle was already raging on the ground, and snipers were shooting at them as they dropped.

Helpless to do anything but pray that no bullets hit him, he looked around at the others. PDX was closest to him and he could see that her body had gone limp. She was dead in the air.

Steve and the others finally made it safe to the ground and were immediately engaged as they tried to get their harnesses off. Steve got his off quickly and immediately took cover beside a nearby shack. He watched while the others removed their harnesses and quickly took cover as well. Zingo tripped and fell as he ran for cover and as a result was shot twice in the side.

"ZINGO!" Steve heard over the commotion. He looked over and saw Blue running over to where Zingo lay on the ground. Just beyond where Blue came from, Steve could see Onion holding on to PDX's limp body.

"BLUE, NO!" Screamed Mudsnake. Blue either didn't hear or was ignoring it and made it out to the injured Zingo. Blue grabbed Zingo's jacket and began to drag him back to cover.

Blue dragged Zingo over to the shack where Steve was. As they approached Steve could see that it was bad. Blood was running from Zingo's mouth. Blue laid Zingo on the ground, instructing Steve to help, they set to work trying to patch him up.

Steve noticed that not only had Zingo taken two shots to the side, but he had also taken one to the leg. Noticing this, Blue instructed Steve.

"Rub some dirt on it."

"Do what?" Asked Steve.

"The dirt helps slow the flow of blood so it can coagulate easier." Blue said. "So just do it."

Steve did as he was instructed, and all the while kept an eye on the others. Onion was still holding PDX, which affected Steve deeply. He had bonded the most with those two, and were like a family within the family of the G.A.A.

Mudsnake and Hall were in a heated discussion on the other side of the road. Buggy, Fuzzy and Juggs had taken up positions on either side of the road and were providing cover fire.

"*FUCK.*" Steve heard Blue yell.

Steve looked back at what he was doing.

"Zingo's dead."

* * *

At Mudsnake's insistance, they all regrouped at one side of the road. There was a plan. Steve and Mudsnake were going to take up positions on both sides of the road, to provide cover with their sniper rifles. Buggy, Fuzzy, and Juggs were going to go up one side of the road, while Onion, Hall, and Blue went up the other.

Steve took up his position, laid down, and looked through his scope. He watched as Buggy, Fuzzy, and Juggs inched their way forward. Moving his aim upwards he caught a glimpse of one of the KEQ soldiers, setting up with a rifle in one of the upper windows of the facility. Steve took careful aim and squeezed the trigger. The soldiers head practically exploded with the force of the impact. Being the comms man, Steve was usually out of the heat of battle so this was the first time Steve had killed anyone.

"I GOT ONE." Steve shouted. "I GOT ONE OF THOSE TURD BURGLERS."

Steve looked over at Mudsnake. Mudsnake was laughing and gave him a thumb's up. When Mudsnake turned back to his rifle, Steve saw the back of his head come apart.

"MUDSNAKE'S DOWN!" Steve yelled over the radio.

Turning back to his own weapon, he watched as Buggy and Fuzzy were both blown to pieces by a grenade. Juggs was also injured in the blast, and was laying on the ground in pain. Steve was about to run and help her when suddenly a KEQ soldier ran up and cut her throat.

Steve quickly took aim and put one of his rounds in the man's chest, killing him instantly. He got up and ran to the other side of the road. Taking cover next to Mudsnake's body, he surveyed that side of the road.

Hall and Blue were both dead in the road, and Onion was taking cover behind a jeep. Steve ran over to her as quick as he could.

"You OK?" He asked.

He could see tear trails in the dirt on her face.

"Is everyone else dead?" She asked.

"Yes." Steve replied.

They waited for a moment trying to figure out what to do, when another plane appeared. More soldiers began jumping out. They landed on the other side of the facility, and within seconds the entire battle shifted to that side of the building.

"They must think we're all dead." Onion said to Steve.

"Let's go." He replied.

They made their way towards the building, picking their way through the debris and bodies. After making it inside, they pulled out a small map, consulted it, then made their way to the center of the facility.

When they found the control room, Steve went inside while Onion guarded the door. Steve slipped his pack off his back and pulled out the explosives inside. He began planting charges around the room.

Onion stuck her head in the door. "Hurry up." She whispered. Steve just smiled at her and continued what he was doing. Suddenly gunfire erupted in ther corridor and Onion staggered inside holding her stomach. She collapsed on the floor and Steve could see four places where bullets had passed through her jacket. Steve set the timer and ran to the door.

He quickly peaked outside and saw a squad of soldiers coming up the hallway. Steve slammed the door shut and braced it with his body. He kept his eyes on the timer. When it reached ten seconds he stepped away from the door.

Nine.

He walked away from the door.

Eight.

He walked over to the far wall.

Seven.

He waited.

Six.

The door burst open.

Five.

A bullet tore into his leg as the squad of soldiers entered the room.

Four.

Two bullets ripped through the flesh of his chest.

Three.

Steve fell to the ground.

Two.

He watched as one of the men put a bullet into Onion's head.

One.

One of the men walked over to Steve and shot him in the chest three times.

Zero.

A massive explosion tore the building apart.

# The Final Curtain

*By Tom*

Forsaken.

Forgotten.

Betrayed.

I am a hollow shell, bruised and beaten, crushed and defeated.

What once was whole, now lies in pieces.

What once had meaning, now makes no sense.

My path is now unclear, clouded and cluttered with uncertainty and doubt.

At one time, everything seemed to have purpose.

Love was my ally,

Friends and family my reward.

But things as they say, never last.

Happiness has an expiration date.

In a burst of flames and a cloud of ash it was stolen from me.

Taken without mercy.

Perhaps I was too content.

Too comfortable.

Now I ride in the back seat with sorrow, a passenger to grief and heartache.

No longer can I smile.

No longer do I have an answer to "What's wrong?", when there is no right.

I can not run from the pain, and I can not hide from the inevitable.

There is no escape.

Only a solution.

A path.

An ending.

They call it cowardice.

A refusal to accept reality.

I can not agree.

These are not obstacles to overcome.
No lesson can be learned.
Silver linings and pots of gold exist only in fairy tales.
Silly stories to vanquish the evil and doubt of our nightmares.
I am alone.
But not for long.
I have found my escape.
My reprieve.
Not through a barrel at point blank range.
No sip from a glass of tainted wine.
I have chosen the purest of exits.
A heroic The End to a story that never read Happily Ever After.

And now, as I stand on the edge of the rail, a footstep away from the crushing yet beautiful waves below, I feel strangely at peace.

This is the only way.

I feel myself smiling, as I raise both arms out like an eagle before the take off.

The rain pours off my body, cold and uncomfortable as it seeps through my clothing, yet refreshing as it awakens my senses.

This is what I must do.

I inhale the sweet, crisp air as it fills my lungs.

I close my eyes and let the cool breeze wash over me, soothing the distant nerves that threaten to shake me.

I look down at my bare feet, delicately gripping the cold, wet steel railing beneath them, awaiting their command to let go.

My heart tells me it is time, ready to part ways into the world beyond.

I glance down once more, hypnotized by the power and beauty below me.

Each wave an outstretched hand.

Each flash of lightning an incandescent beacon lighting the way.

It's time.

I take in one final gulp of air, and raise my right foot into the air, my knee level with my waist.

Closing my eyes, I extend it into the air, and take a step into th-

"Annnnnnnnnnnd cut!"

Lights sprang to life as the actor froze, balanced on the railing of a stage prop.

"Now what?" he called out.

The director got up from his seat in the empty and darkened auditorium, and made his way to the edge of the stage.

"Nothing," he replied. "It's perfect. Well done."

The actor jumped down and began walking across the stage.

"You really think we're gonna win 'em over with this?" he asked.

"Win them over?" the director exclaimed. "This scene is pure power, mark my words. When the final curtain falls, there won't be a dry eye in the house."

# Joey : Part 1

*By Chris*

Hi.

Let me introduce myself.

My name is Joey.

I'm five years old and this is my story so far.

I'm not really sure where to start. So I will start with the first things I can remember. The earliest memories I have are of two people. Mommy and Daddy.

The first memory I have, I think I was around three. I was upstairs with Mommy while she was doing some cleaning when someone knocked on the door downstairs. I got very excited and ran to the top of the stairs but I ran too fast and ended up sliding right off the edge and tumbled all the way down the stairs. Mommy came running down the stairs when she heard me crying. She picked me up as she sat down, she held me in her arms, hugging me and rubbing my head to make me feel better. The knock came a couple more times, but Mommy never even went to see who was there.

Later that night, after Daddy came home, we all had dinner; I sat on the couch with them all night as they watched TV. They loved me. I know they did. But a couple years later things started to change.

I can't tell you when exactly the changes began to take place, but things happened really quickly. It was just after I turned five. I started to notice that Mommy was staying home more often. Not only was she staying home though, but she was also staying in bed a lot. Most days I would lay with her, but after a while she began to smell funny. It was like it was her but also another smell of something bad inside of her.

After a while Daddy started staying home a lot too. On the days when he was home I wasn't allowed to be in bed with Mommy, Daddy made me stay in the other room. I didn't get to spend those days with Mommy, but after Mommy went to sleep, I would get to sit with Daddy on the couch. A lot of these times when it was just us, he would talk to me and cry. I never understood what he was saying but I tried to be there for him.

One day the smell was really strong in the house and Daddy was really upset. There were two strangers in the house and they were taking Mommy outside on a rolling bed. I tried to give her a kiss, but the bed was too high and the strangers had her face covered with a blanket.

Daddy went out after the strangers left and never came home that night. When he came home the next night he smelled funny too. It wasn't the same smell as Mommy, this was different. Something was wrong with him because he was walking funny too. He started yelling at me right away for making a mess in the house, but I was only five years old and I had never been left alone overnight before. He lay down on the couch, and when I tried to get up with him he pushed me off.

The next day Daddy smelled funny again. He must have been really thirsty too, because he was always drinking something. The phone rang, and Daddy was standing by the sink talking. He started crying again so I went over as he hung the phone up. He looked down at me, and then just walked away. I followed him as he walked up the stairs. When he saw that I was following him, he turned around and pushed me down the stairs with his foot and told me to get lost. I started crying when I hit the bottom but this time no one was there to comfort me.

I missed Mommy.

When Daddy came down I was scared, but I was also hungry. It had been two days since I had something to eat. I asked him for some food but it only made him madder. He picked me up and walked to the door. He opened the door, and walked outside. He put me down on the ground and then turned around and went back inside.

That was the last time I ever saw Daddy.

I spent two days outside by myself. On the first day I stayed close to home, hoping that Daddy would come out, take me in the house and love me again. The next day I was too hungry to wait for him and began to wander around looking for food. I found some on the ground by some outside tables. I picked it up and ran down an alley and ate it.

Some men came a while later. They were very nice. They picked me up, and took me to their car. I was scared but at the same time I was excited. Scared because they were strangers, but excited because they were being nice to me. After a short drive we got to a big building. They picked me up and took me inside.

One of the men held me while they talked with a lady at a desk. After a few minutes they took me to a room where there was a man in a white coat. The other men sat me on a table and then left. The new man began to look at me and touch me all over. It was a little scary but he was nice to me too and never hurt me at all.

After that I was taken and put into a room by myself for a while. I was alone but at least they brought me food. Lots of food. I ate until I was stuffed, and then slept. After a couple of days, I was feeling a lot better. Some other men took me back to the man in the white coat. He touched me lots again, but again he was very nice. After he was done I was taken to a different room.

I don't know how long I was in this new room but people would walk by me everyday. Sometimes they would stop and say "Hi." but mostly they would just look at me and keep going.

Then one day a big person was walking with a little person and they stopped.

"I like this one." Said the little person.

"Let me see." The big one said as he pulled a piece of paper from the door of my room. "This says, Hello, my name is Joey, I am a five year old Jack Russell Terrier."

"I like him." The little one stated again.

"O.K. Buddy." Said the big one as he put the paper back on my door. "Let's go to the office and see if they will let us take him home."

As they walked away, two things kept repeating in my mind. The little one called the big one "Daddy" and the big one said "Home".

Hi.

My name is Joey.

I am a Jack Russell Terrier.

I am getting a second chance.

# According To You
*By Chris*

Dear Mom.

    I am writing this so that you will have some answers as to why I have done what I have done. I know that you will only disagree with everything I say here, but I need to speak my mind and God knows I can't say anything to your face. First off, don't worry about baby Edward. He's somewhere safe. I didn't want him to be here for this.

    So anyway let me begin.

    According to you I have always been nothing but a spoiled little girl. You claim that I have always had everything I wanted handed to me, but the truth is Mom, that I have worked my ass off for everything I have. Even when I was younger, whenever I wanted something, you would make me work for it. Yes you did give me things and do things for me when I was very young, but ever since I was eight it was different. That was when you told me I had to grow up and start being responsible.

    I remember the first thing you did was teach me how to cook. I remember I caught on fast. Then I was the one cooking dinner every night. At eight years old. No other kid my age was doing that. When they were all getting called in from outside for supper, I was calling you into the kitchen from the living room for supper. Not only did I cook, but you made me clean everything up afterwards. When everyone else was going back outside to play I was busy cleaning up the kitchen, washing dishes, and washing the floor.

    According to you I have always been nothing but a dirty little slob. Every night I would have a bath, wash up, get into my jammies, and then go and see you with the hairbrush. You would brush my hair for me every night. Do you remember the special bonding time we had Mom? You calling me names like dirty and filthy while ripping the brush through my hair while I stood there with tears pouring out and soaking the front of my jammy shirt. Do you remember the time you were pulling so hard that the brush actually snapped in my hair? I do.

I tried my best to be the clean little girl you always wanted. I always tried to keep myself clean by not playing on grass or mud, or running just in case I would fall. I remember the time a boy named Austin pushed me down outside and I got mud on my dress. Do you remember that? I do. I was so scared that I ran to my room and changed and hid the dress from you. I remember you were too drunk to notice but you found the dress the next day while I was at school. Do you remember what you did? I do. Do you remember what we had for dinner that night? I do. You had a plate of pasta that I made you but I wasn't allowed to have any. Is this ringing any bells Mom? When I asked you what I was having for supper you handed me a bowl of mud from the garden and told me to eat that. I remember I told you no, but you insisted that if I didn't eat that, then I was eating nothing. You smacked me then. Remember? Knocked me right off my feet. Then you got next to me on the floor and started shoving the mud into my mouth. Do you remember Mom? I do.

According to you I was nothing but trouble. Always being a brat and getting into trouble. I remember one time I borrowed a doll from the neighbor kid across the street. I don't remember her name, and it doesn't really matter anyway because it wasn't her name that hurt. She had come to the door to ask for it back and it was you who answered. You were nice enough to her and asked her to wait while you went and got it. I heard you, I was waiting in my doorway with it. Do you remember Mom? I do. You grabbed that doll from my hands and then swung it at me, making my nose bleed. Do you remember Mom? I do. I was ten.

Do you remember how you used to punish me when you thought I was misbehaving? Do you remember the corner Mom? I do. Every time I was in trouble and you were finished hitting me you would put me in the corner. Face into the corner, but I wasn't allowed to stand up, was I Mom? No, you made me stay on my knees with my feet off the floor. Do you know how much that hurt? Or what was worse was when my legs got tired and my feet did touch the floor. Do you remember what happened then Mom? I do. You had a coathanger that you had straightened out. When you would catch my feet on the floor you would whip the soles of my feet with it. Sometimes if you were too drunk you would miss my feet and hit the back of my thighs, my butt, or my back.

Do you remember the punishment in the winter Mom? I do. You used to take me to the back door, remember? That was where you would strip me down to my underwear and then take me outside. Do you remember Mom. I do. You would make me lay down in the snow and roll around while I counted to one hundred. I remember I wasn't allowed to count fast, or I had to start over.

According to you, as soon as I hit puberty and started getting boobs I was nothing but a slut. I remember one time watching the kids outside playing through a window. You walked in and said all I was doing was thinking about the boys. Laying with the boys. Spreading my legs for the boys. I had no idea what any of that meant at the time. That didn't matter, I remember you grabbed me by the hair and broke my nose on the window sill. Do you remember that Mom? I do.

I remember you having a new boyfriend almost every week too Mom. Do you? You made me call every single one of them Daddy. Remember that? I do. "Get Daddy a beer. Make Daddy some food. Go wash Daddy's laundry." Do you remember making me do all those things? I do. I tried to hide in my room as much as I could when you had company, but you used to make me come out so you could pretend to be 'Mommy Of The Year'. "Come sit on Daddy's lap and watch T.V. with us." Do you remember saying that? I remember hearing that tons of times. Do you have any idea how many of those guys copped a feel when you got up to get more beer, or go to the bathroom? I do. All of them did it. I don't know what you expected, you would pick them up at the bar and they would only last until the next one caught your fancy.

How do you think I became pregnant at thirteen? It was Dale. Not a boy at school like I told you. You thought he was great. Kept him around for a whole month. I think the only reason he stayed around so long was because when he was done with you and you passed out he would come into my room and make me do things. Do you remember what you did when I told you about it Mom? I do. You called me a liar and smashed your beer bottle across my mouth. That one cost me four teeth and twenty six stitches. Remember what you told them at the hospital Mom? I do. You told them I was playing baseball and got hit with the bat. They believed you too.

The reason I am bringing all this up is because I want you to know that you absolutely destroyed my life. I'm fourteen years old and there is nothing left inside of my soul that isn't broken in some way. You have taken every fibre of my being and pulled me apart piece by piece.

Something happened last week that I need to tell you about. It was the day Edward turned a month old. I remember I had just gotten in another argument with you. You had left to go to the bar and I was getting some ice so my eye wouldn't swell too badly. In the other room Edward started crying, so I went in, picked him up and tried to sooth him. He wouldn't stop crying for anything. I laid him back in his crib, went to the closet, grabbed a coathanger and straightened it out. I rushed back to the crib and at the last second stopped myself. One month old and I was going to do to him what you had done to me. I dropped the hanger and fell down and cried. That was when I understood what needed to be done.

I have written letters to the police, the newspaper, and every relative I could think of. I told them almost everything that I have said to you here. Hopefully the police come for you. I really hope they do. But more than that. I hope you never see Edward again. I know I won't. That hurts me. The one joy I do have is that I won't have to spend another day with you.

If all goes right, You will find this letter, then you will find my body in the bathtub. I hope the image of all the blood stays with you forever.

Goodbye Mom.

Your Dirty Little Troublemaking Slut,

Lisa.

# Hope

*By Chris*

She gently floated out of her dream-filled slumber, awakening in the darkened room. She laid flat on her back, listening to the sound of her own deep breaths, memories of the night's activities still drifting in fragments through her mind.

Her eyes slowly began to adjust in the darkness and after a moment she was able to make out details of things about the room. The large mirror on the wall to her left, the dresser in the far corner of the room, the chair near the desk; she could even see the clothes strewn around the bedroom floor.

She rolled over and looked at him. Laying there sleeping, he was a far cry from the passionate lovemaking machine he had turned out to be earlier. Now, he looked more like a young boy who was totally at peace with the world around him. She watched the steady rise and fall of his chest as his lungs inhaled the chilly night air coming in through the window.

The flesh on her arm and thighs raised up with goose bumps as a cool breeze blew through the room. He grabbed the blanket in his sleep and pulled it up tight to his chin and rolled over with his back to her. Her heart fluttered in her chest when she thought of the raw, carnal emotions she had felt earlier.

She gently slid to the edge of the bed and slowly sat up so not to wake him. As she sat, she idly massaged the carpet with her toes, her thoughts once again turned to the passion that was alive in her just a little while ago.

When she finally stood, the bed expressed a soft squeak of relief. She began to walk to the door, when she suddenly stopped. Something had caught her eye while she walked but she soon realized it was her own reflection in the mirror as she walked across the shadowy room.

She paused and took a long look at herself. She could not really see much but her own silhouette. She turned this way and that, looking at herself from different angles.

She thought about stopping to find her clothes, but decided against it. It would take too long and besides, they were alone in the house so no one was around to care if she was naked or not.

She made her way out into the hall and walked to the top of the stairs. A light was on downstairs, and as she descended she could make out the pictures on the walls. Family pictures mostly. Nothing really stood out in her mind to give her a sense of who he really was.

When she got to the bottom of the stairs, she found his shirt lying in a heap. She stooped, picked it up, and held it to her face. She inhaled deeply, breathing in all the essence of him. A smile crept to the corners of her mouth as she let the shirt fall away from her hands and back down to the floor.

She sighed to herself as she looked at the shirt lying on the floor.

Is this love? She asked herself.

No.

It was too soon.

Or was it?

It was hard to tell. She thought she had been in love once before, but that....

Forget it. She told herself. It's old news.

It may have been old news but the wounds were still so fresh that she vowed never to let herself fall for another man.

Suddenly, panic overtook her. What if she was falling in love? What if she let herself get drawn in deep emotionally?

Not knowing what to do, she quickly but quietly made her way back up the stairs. She entered the bedroom and began picking up every article of clothing she could find. She bundled it all into a ball in her arms and rushed back down the stairs.

When she got downstairs and into the light she began to sort through the clothing. She put her own on as she tossed his aside. She pulled up her jeans, threw her shirt on inside out.

Home, she thought. I've got to get home.

Tears were streaming down her face as she made her way to the front door. She could taste the salt on her lips as she wiped the tears away with her trembling hands.

This is love, it had to be, otherwise she wouldn't be acting the way she was. She sat down on the oak preachers' bench he kept near the front door. She had to think, had to convince herself to be sensible about the whole thing.

She looked to where her shoes were, not two feet away. I could go, she thought. It would be easy, slide the shoes onto her feet, walk out the door and never look back.

For months she had nursed a tiny, harmless crush on him. He had asked her out a couple of times but she had warily told him no on each occasion. Two weeks ago at a mutual friends house, they had both become kind of tipsy and wound up having a minor make out session near the end of the night.

For days afterward the knowledge of that make out session gnawed at her. Part of her regretted ever going to that party but the other part was happy that feelings were finally coming out into the open.

For the next two weeks, barely a word was spoken between the two even though they saw each other almost daily. They shared the knowing glances, but neither one of them wanted to be the one to mention what had happened. She wanted to talk to him, let him know it was a mistake, but when she searched her true feelings she knew it wasn't a mistake and only wanted more.

He was the one who broke the silence. He had called her two days ago and asked her if she wanted to go for dinner. She had tried to tell him no but her mouth deceived her and she had accepted. They had agreed to meet at a restaurant for dinner and possibly head out to a movie afterward.

Dinner was supposed to be at six, and as she was getting ready to leave there was a very soft knock at her door. She opened the door and was caught by surprise at the sight of a little girl holding a bunch of roses. The girl appeared to be around five or six years old, and was wearing a beautiful pink dress. The girl held the roses out for her, and when she took them the little girl let out a giggle, turned and ran down the walk.

When the girl was out of sight, she went back inside and closed the door. She held the flowers close and breathed in the overwhelming scent. She walked toward the kitchen still smelling them as she went. Hunting through her cabinets she found an old vase. She looked at the clock, and, deciding there was still some time set about cutting and arranging them.

Just as she was finishing up she had noticed that there were eleven flowers in the bunch. She walked down the hall towards the door thinking maybe she had dropped one on the way when there was another knock on the door. She opened it and there he was, holding a single rose in his hand.

"I believe you are missing one," he said.

She ushered him into the house, taking the flower from him. She went back to the kitchen and added the single flower to the arrangement she had done.

"Are you ready for dinner?" He asked.

"Yes." She replied.

She gathered up her purse and they exited the house together. Idle chat was made as they walked to his car. He walked her to the passenger side of the car and opened the door for her. She slipped into the seat and he carefully closed the door.

"So where are we going?" She asked as he climbed into the drivers' seat.

"Nowhere special," he replied as he started the engine and backed down the driveway.

Disappointment hit her like a ton of bricks when he had said that. The night had seemed to start off so special and now they were going 'nowhere special' for dinner. She tried not to let it show and she wasn't sure if she should even be expecting more. When they made plans top go out he had said just to dress casual so maybe she was expecting too much.

When they pulled up in front of his house she questioned why they were there and he had said that he had forgotten something. He asked if she would like to come in for a second and she had agreed out of curiosity.

When they entered the dimly lit foyer, she was struck by the wonderful aroma of something cooking. They took off their shoes and he led her to the dining room where she found a table that was beautifully set with candles, flowers and food.

"Shall we?" He asked with a boyish grin.

Embarrassed by her thoughts earlier she could only nod as she felt her face flush. He held the chair for her as she sat then he turned and went to his own seat across the table.

They settled in and ate their dinner and drank their wine over wonderful conversation. Nothing was mentioned about what had happened between them previously with both of them avoiding the subject all through dinner. The food was absolutely delicious and when she commented on it he had told her that he had prepared it earlier so he was glad she enjoyed it.

When dinner was finished they retired to the living room with the bottle of wine. Looking around the room she noticed his DVD collection and asked if he wanted to watch one. He agreed so she picked out a comedy thinking she would try to keep the mood light.

Halfway through the movie she asked him to pause it so she could use the washroom. He did and she did. When she came back she sat closer to him than she had been and snuggled up under his arm. He seemed a little surprised by her but it didn't take long for him to adjust.

When the movie was finished he asked if she was ready for him to take her home. She replied by kissing him long and deep.

"I want to stay." She whispered, her lips still very close to his.

"Are you sure?" He asked.

She kissed him again. "Yes," she replied.

She stood, and grabbing him by the hand led him out of the room. When they reached the stairs leading up to the bedroom, she pushed him up against the wall and kissed him again. This time letting her hands explore his body. She raised his shirt over his head and tossed it aside. She then turned and walked up the stairs. He stood watching her from the bottom of the stairs, as she reached the door to his bedroom he saw her remove her own shirt and that was when he followed.

He caught her inside the door and pulled her close. They kissed again, all the while tearing at each others clothes.

The sex was great. At first that's what she had thought it was, just sex. Sitting here now, contemplating walking out, she wondered to herself if there was more to it. Maybe there was something there.

When they were together, she felt like the rest of the world didn't even exist. In that time and space it was just the two of them. All the pressures and frustrations of life had just seemed to peel away like layers, leaving them with nothing but raw emotion and feeling.

She sat there, thinking. She wanted to find love, and if this was it she didn't want to let it pass her by. At the same time the fear of getting hurt again was starting to creep in like an unwelcome visitor who just wouldn't leave.

She thought of him, lying in the bed upstairs. How wonderful it was being with him.

If she walked out now she would never know what could be.

His touch.

Heartbreak.

His tenderness.

Pain.

His love.

She stood. Turning away from the shoes at the door, she made her way back up the stairs.

She had made her decision.

She had to try, to trust.

She undressed and slipped back into the room and climbed in bed with him.

Feeling her coming back in, he rolled over, got up on one elbow and asked. "Everything o.k.?"

She leaned into him and gave him another deep kiss. "I hope so."

# I Don't Love You Anymore

*By Chris*

His head was pounding, his body ached and he was unable to sit up. He waited a few more seconds and tried again. He made it into a sitting position and looked around. The alley was dark and empty as far as he could tell. His assailants must have grown tired or bored of beating him.

*I don't love you anymore.*

Those words echoed through his head. Struggling to get to his feet, he stumbled and backed himself into the wall. Next to him was the door through which he was half carried and half thrown.

He kicked the door. "Fuck you!" He yelled.

The thumping of the music resounding through the door made him positive that no one heard his little rant. He stumbled off down the alley towards Main Street.

When he got to the sidewalk he turned left and walked towards a bus stop that was close by. He kind of half sat and half fell onto the bench causing a shot of pain to shoot through his side. He was no doctor but assumed that this was what broken ribs must feel like.

He reached into his pocket and pulled out a crumpled pack of smokes. Opening it, he was disappointed to find that every last one had been either broken or crushed. Picking one out, he broke off the filter and stuck it in his mouth. He had never smoked a filterless cigarette before but he figured now was as good a time as any to try one. Pulling out his lighter he was struck by the inscription on it.

*My fire will always burn for you.*

He laughed and tossed it into a nearby trash can.

*Only until this morning, right bitch?* He thought.

He lit the flame and held it to the smoke. Inhaling deeply, the smoke was stronger than he expected causing a coughing fit to start. Tears filled his eyes as pain racked his body from his presumedly broken ribs. He tossed the smoke away and laid on the bench.

*I don't love you anymore.*

The five words that started the whole mess.

Laying there waiting for the bus the day began to replay itself through his mind.

* * *

He had woken up this morning anticipating that it was going to be a great day. After all, it was his birthday. April 1st, 2011, the day he turned thirty. He looked over to see that Jenny wasn't in bed with him.

*Shame.* He thought.

Would have been nice to start the day with a good old romp in the sack, but it looked like today the morning wood was going to go to waste.

He got out of the bed and made his way to the bathroom. He turned the shower on and hopped in. Maybe Jenny would hear the water running and decide to hop in with him.

She never came.

He dried off, went into the bedroom to get dressed, then made his way out into the kitchen.

When he saw her sitting at the table, he could tell something wasn't right. The look on her face stopped him dead in his tracks. She looked at him standing in the doorway and he could see tears welling up in her eyes.

She stood.

Tears were flowing freely now.

"I don't love you anymore." She said to him.

She didn't wait for a response. She picked up a suitcase sitting by the table, and without looking back, walked down the hall and out the door.

Even if she had waited for him to say something, she would've waited a long time. He was at a loss for words. He just stood there dumbfounded. After what seemed like an eternity, he left the doorway and sat down at the table.

* * *

He stood up as the bus approached. He grabbed a couple bucks from his pocket and waited as the bus came to a stop in front of him. When he stepped up to deposit his money, the look on the bus driver's face told him that he must look worse than he felt. And he felt pretty shitty.

With no other passengers to worry about, he chose a seat near the middle of the bus. He sat and looked out the window as it began to move.

* * *

After she had left, he waited a while then headed down to Mike's, the bar on the corner of Main Street and Orchard Avenue. It was a twenty minute walk, but he felt he needed it. He needed to do something. Sitting at the table, all he could think of were those five words and wonder what had caused them to be spoken.

They had their arguments, sure, but everybody does. They weren't anything particularly nasty and never lasted very long. As far as he could figure it, there was absolutely no reason for her to throw away the two years like she had.

Unless there was someone else.

That was it.

It had to be.

By the time he got to the bar, he was no longer feeling sorry for himself, now he was just pissed off.

That fucking bitch. How dare she go out and have someone else behind his back. How many times had he kissed her after she came home from blowing someone else? Who knows what was on those lips. If he ever saw her again, he decided, it would be too soon.

He walked up to the bar and ordered a shot of Jack. He downed it as soon as it was handed to him, and he ordered another. His plan was to get drunk. Very, very drunk.

After this, his memory began to get a bit fuzzy. He remembered sitting at the bar. There were about twenty other people in the tiny place. Some were sitting at the bar but most were gathered around the two pool tables in the back. He had gotten up to take a leak and while walking to the bathroom he had bumped into a woman while she was lining up a shot at the table.

"Hey!" She had said.

He laughed at her and just kept on walking.

After finishing his business, he was on his way back over to the bar and bumped into the same woman again, this time on purpose. As he walked away she jabbed him in the back with the pool cue. He spun on her angrily, "You fucking whore!" he shouted as he lunged at her.

That was his mistake, taking his misguided anger out on a woman he didn't even know. Four guys, maybe five grabbed him before he could reach her and proceded to drag him out the back door. They took him into the back alley, threw him on the ground and beat him unconscious, and that was where he woke up.

* * *

The bus came to a stop in front of his building and he proceded to get off. He could hear the bus fading away in the distance as he unlocked the building door and made his way inside.

*I don't love you anymore.*

Those words were going to haunt him for the rest of his life.

He made it to his apartment, unlocked the door and stepped inside.

When he flicked on the light he was greeted by a room full of people.

"Surprise!" They all exclaimed. After that single word was shouted the room went dead quiet as people took in the sight of him.

There was a banner hanging in the back of the room that said *Happy Birthday.*

Standing in front of him in the center of the room was Jenny. She was holding her own sign. This one read, *April fools baby, I do love you!*

# Lucky Socks

*By Tom*

I don't know who invented socks.

Frankly, I don't care.

It's not as if I'm not appreciative of the fact they exist.

They keep our feet warm.

They...well, that's about it.

They don't look good.

They're not fashionable.

A man can get a slap in the jaw for wearing them with sandals.

So what's the big deal about them?

You can't use them as part of a pick-up line.

"Yeah, you think the suit looks good? Well...let your peepers get a gander at these foot warmers. Fruit of the Loom, baby!"

And say it starts to work? How would you close the deal?

"You like? Well, my dear, you should come back to my place. I've got a drawer full of 'em."

No, sadly, that's never going to happen.

If it were, I wouldn't be complaining.

And holy hell, look at all the choices!

You've got socks made out of cotton, wool, nylon and polyester.

A sub-sock group actually designed specifically for legs, knees, ankles and yes, even toes.

And then, just for kicks, a sub-sub-sock group composed of thousands and thousands of different designs and colours.

And the funny part?

You know the people behind this entire operation are sitting on a beach with their bare feet in the sand, laughing while they count their money and sip on margaritas, all the while looking at one another and saying, "Those poor bastards will buy anything!"

And do you ever notice it's always the senior citizens of the world who seem most likely to fall prey to the trend?

Yes, comrades, this means our dear Grandmas and Grandpas.

Whether they're in a package of six or hand knitted with love, who deemed it appropriate to wrap socks up in paper, throw a ribbon on it and say *Merry Christmas!* as it's handed to a loved one?

Thanks Grandma, don't mind me while I just choke myself out with last year's pair.

Take me for example.

I'm a couple days short of twenty.

Nineteen years ago, my Grandma Sue came down with a nasty case of *What was she thinking?*

Her symptoms?

Coming to the decision that her grandson was never going to have his feet go cold.

She knitted wool socks.

Tube socks.

Red socks.

Blue socks.

I did not like them, Sam I am, I did not like those socks from Gram.

Every Christmas.

Every Easter.

Every birthday.

Every damn day she could get away with.

I remember my tenth birthday.

I remember the socks.

Grey, double-layered wool socks with white and red horizontal stripes.

Awful. Dear God were they awful.

It might have been the feeling of superiority in owning two digits in my age, or possibly the amount of sugar I had consumed in cookies, cake and ice cream, but it was while getting ready for bed later that night that I decided to have a sit down with my mother.

"Mommy, is Grandma crazy?"

"Crazy? What are you talking about sweetie?"

I stood there, clothed in my new birthday suit: Blue and white Toronto Maple Leafs pyjamas with a picture of Mats Sundin celebrating a goal plastered on the shirt.

I looked badass.

In one hand I held a new Power Rangers toy and in the other, the socks.

"Mommy," I said, holding up the new toy. "This is a good birthday present."

She looked at me, confused but intrigued. She smiled in spite of herself.

"I'm glad you liked it, Michael. But what does that have to do with Grandma?"

"Well," I said, holding up the socks in front of me like a slimy banana peel that had been sitting for days in the sun. "This is not a good birthday present."

"Michael Christian Mathers! Explain yourself!"

"Mommy," I explained, looking up at her, "Grandma always gives me socks. All the time. Is she crazy? Or does she not like me?"

My mother bent down on knee, grabbed my new gifts, placed them on the bed, and grabbed my hands in hers.

"Michael, your Grandma loves you very much. She takes a lot of time with those socks. She makes them all herself, and puts a lot of effort and love into every pair."

Sure.

I bought it.

I was ten.

I still believed that the Tooth Fairy gave me two bucks instead of one because her and my grandpa went to school together.

But a decade and hundreds of socks later, enough was enough.

It was talk time again.

It was the night before my teen years were behind me, and I found my mother in the den, tying helium birthday balloons together in groups of three.

"Hey, Mom."

My mother, too deep in concentration, barely looked up from what she was doing, instead nodded and gave me a half smile in acknowledgment.

She was not the kind of woman who gave in to tradition and holiday cheer the way some moms did, but when it came to birthdays in our house, she turned into Martha Stewart faster than you could blow out a candle.

My older brother Frankie and I were powerless to the will of Birthday Mom.

And if either one of us attempted to stand up and fight back against her say-so?

Well...let's not open up those scars again.

Let's just say getting shot, stabbed or punched did less damage than a bathtub photo or bed-wetting tale.

Whenever we'd ask her why she kept up with the birthday madness year after year, she merely responded, "It's the one day where I get to celebrate the 'gift' of you to the world!"

And then she'd grab us in hugs and sob on our shoulders.

A sad sight to behold, indeed.

So, rather than protest and remind my mother that I was turning twenty, I avoided my inevitable demise and sat down next to her.

"What's up, sweetie?" she asked, the balloon string between her teeth.

"Nothing. I just wanted to talk to you about something."

"Shoot."

I paused, resisting the urge to shout out, "Don't invite Grandma!"

Don't get me wrong.

I love my grandma more than anything.

She's always been a strong woman, a loving wife, mother of five children and many, many grandchildren.

When I was still a wee lad, my grandfather passed away and, not wanting to be alone, my grandmother stepped up to look after me, my brother and all my other cousins.

We used to spend our summers at her house while our parents were at work.

She taught us how to play card games like euchre; and then she cheated to beat us.

She tried teaching us about flowers and how to grow things like tomatoes and cucumbers out of the garden.

I might add that she quickly gave up after discovering we cared more about eating them.

Me and my brother used to tell our parents, "There's no place like home...except when we're at Grandma's."

My grandmother's living proof that where some homes rested on dirt, cement and wood, our home, our family, rested upon her.

So, keeping all of that in mind, I looked into my mother's eyes and said, "We need to have a talk about Grandma."

She looked up, a look of curiosity on her face. "OK?"

I gently grabbed the strings out of her hands, causing three balloons to float slowly to the ceiling.

"Is something wrong, Mikey?"

"Well…not really. I'm not sure where to start, actually."

"Just say it, honey. Spill the beans."

I sighed, taking in a deep breath and holding it for all it was worth.

"Idunwannhertbrinmesocksagan!"

My mother just stared, a bewildered look on her face.

"Alright…well, let's try this again…in English, please, Michael?"

"I'm sorry, just nervous."

"That was nerves?" she said, smiling. "Sounded more like Tarantino trying to speak human for the first time."

As if to confirm her suspicion, Tarantino, our eight-year-old Siamese cat strolled by, staring up at me with his mischievous little yellow eyes, as if to say *don't even think about laughing, asshole*.

"Funny," I said impatiently. "But no. I kind of just wanted to express my…distaste…of a certain someone's…gifts?"

As i suspected, her eyes narrowed with warning, aware I was probably going to say something she didn't like.

"This is about the socks, Michael?"

I hesitated. Nodded.

"Michael, we've had this talk before."

"Mom, I was ten. You can't 'have a talk' with a ten-year-old."

"Your grandmother loves you," she said impatiently, looking irritated. "And she puts a lot of time and care into each pair she makes."

"Mom, I remember this argument. And I appreciate the fact she makes them all herself. But are you telling me that for twenty years Grandma's first thought when I would come to mind is: Michael needs socks?"

My mother rolled her eyes.

"Your grandma used to make your grandpa socks all the time, you know. I think she's always seen a bit of him in you."

I had no comeback to that comment.

I was losing my argument before I could even inflict a headshot.

Time to hit the panic button.

"It's not like I don't love that Grandma thinks about me. It's just that...I'm starting college soon, and, I don't know...I don't think that socks will pay my tuition."

"Michael Christian Mathers!' she said, giving me a light slap over the head. "I didn't raise you to be greedy!"

"I'm not greedy!" I replied, trying to make her understand. "I'm just saying, it might be nice if, instead of needling me up some socks, she maybe cuts me a cheque."

"Michael!"

Alright. Maybe I had gone too far.

"Do you know what your grandmother said to me and your father the day we brought you home from the hospital?"

I shook my head.

This wasn't going to be good.

"I placed you in her arms," she told me, "and she started rocking you back and forth. When she looked up at me, she had tears in her eyes. She kissed you on the forehead and whispered something to you. Do you know what she whispered?"

I shook my head again.

*Eject! Eject you fool!*

"She said 'You've brought new life to me little one. I was never really born until you came along.'"

And there it was.

The final punch to the gonads.

Game, set, match.

C'est finis.

Mom, one.

Mike, niente.

I thought I was prepared.

I played dirty, brought a gun to a knife fight.

And my mother had shown up behind the wheel of a tank.

Zero chance of survival.

The best (and only) thing to do now was to sit speechless, look stunned and display my most irritated, defeated face.

Something I've had the bad luck of mastering.

"Is that all then, honey?" My mother said, without looking up. "I've really got to get all of this done before tomorrow."

*Damn you, woman! The nerve! Not enough to beat a man but gotta kick him when he's down!*

"Yeah, that's it I guess."

I stood up, feeling incomprehensibly pathetic and small.

My mommy had just made me feel like I was ten again.

"Oh, Michael one more thing while I have you here?"

I turned to face her, looking less than enthusiastic.

"Do me a favour sweetie. For tomorrow, let Grandma see you in one of the pairs of socks she's given you. Maybe the blue and black ones? Thanks, Mikey."

I gave her a quick smile and a nod before making my way out of the room.

Making sure no one was in eyeshot, I reached down and quickly made a physical scan of my crotchal area.

Yup. Still there.

\* \* \*

Happy Birthday to me.

The big twenty.

Numero...twenty.

I'd been around for two decades.

Battled through infancy, adolescence and the whole "rebellious teenager" phase.

As a child I had prayed to the gods of facial hair for a little fuzz.

And through prayer I had been given not only a fair few bristles, but the tools in which to tame them: A razor and a can of shaving cream.

Yes, I was a man now.

It should have been like Neil Armstrong's first footstep on the moon. A well-placed quote followed by applause and high fives.

Instead, I was stuck at the little kid's table of my own birthday party, wiping spaghetti sauce from my little cousins' chins while listening to them bombard me with an endless amount of alternate punch lines to why the damn chickens kept crossing the road.

And when I try to contribute?

Nothing but tears, screaming and stern looks from my aunts and uncles.

"Grow up, Michael," my Aunt Judy said coldly.

"What did I do?" I asked innocently." They kept telling that chicken crossing the road joke! I just contributed my own punch line."

"Telling them it was because Colonel Sanders chopped all their heads off and they didn't know where they were going is crossing the line. You should know better."

"Sorry."

A knock at the front door gave me the opportunity to escape the snake pit for a few minutes.

Before I could even get there, the knob slowly turned and the door opened wide.

"Happy Birthday Michael!"

I smiled.

"Thanks Grandma."

My grandmother was by no means a spring chicken.

She was average height, with long, straight white hair.

She had a bit of a stoop, and occasionally had to carry a cane when she did groceries or went for a walk.

But she was also by no means an old hen.

She had mysteriously green eyes that made me think of rainforests or the wind blowing through the branches of a tree on a spring morning.

She had a sense of humour to rival marvels like Ellen Degeneres or Lucille Ball.

And the sense of energy she continuously emitted at her age was both baffling and inspiring.

Trust me, I've felt enough pain running away from the end of her wooden spoon to know the woman can move.

"How goes it old man?" she asked, slipping her shoes off, handbag in one hand and walking stick in the other.

"Oh, not so good," I replied. "I woke up craving prune juice. But when I went to check the fridge three minutes later, I forgot what I was doing in the kitchen."

She laughed.

"You know, somehow I thought you might be feeling changes. So I decided to get you something new this year."

I hesitated before replying. Could it be?

"Oh?"

"Oh yes," she replied matter-of-factly. "You ready for it?"

"Yes, ma'am."

She had a look of confusion on her face as she patted the pockets of her pants and sweater. A few seconds later, she had a big smile plastered on her face, the cane in her outstretched hand.

"Judging by your posture, I can see you're going to get some good mileage out of it."

I took the cane in both hands, looking it over the way a pirate looks over a piece of gold.

'I love it Grandma. But does it come in blue?"

She snorted and threw her arms out.

"Come give your elder a hug, good-looking."

I walked into her arms, and she hugged me tightly.

That was one of the many great things about my grandma.

Since we were young, there were two things she never ran out of: hugs and cookies.

Twenty years later and I still looked forward to both.

"I see you're wearing my socks."

We broke apart, both of us staring down at the black and blue speckled socks on my feet.

"Umm...I sure am."

She reached into her handbag and pulled out a small, wrapped package and handed it to me.

"Happy birthday, my angel."

Holding the soft, squishy package in my hand didn't take me long to figure out what hid inside.

I looked up into my grandmother's face to see her brilliantly green eyes brimming with tears of pride and love.

Swallowing back the lump of disappointment, I summoned the biggest smile to my face.

"Thank you Grandma."

Oh, I forgot to mention. I was a coward.

* * *

The rest of the night went at a snail's pace.

Dinner was followed by sitting around the table and talking.

Followed by coffee, birthday cake and talking.

And finally followed by the main event: birthday gifts.

Oh, while talking.

It was a pretty good haul.

Money, clothes, movies, and for some unknown reason, a bag of dog biscuits.

See, I don't own a dog.

The last dog I had was a little chocolate Lab named Henry.

One day we were walking and he got off the leash and took off.

Spent weeks searching for him.

Never found him.

Thanks for bringing up painful memories, Uncle Carl.

Laugh it up.

Your birthday's next month right?

And don't you have peanut allergies?

Can't wait for that party.

So, after many thanks, hugs and, in my uncle's case, a teaspoon of Frank's Red Hot sauce in his evening coffee, I came upon the last gift of the night.

To, my dearest Michael.

Love, Grandma.

I stared at the little package.

I grabbed a piece of paper that wasn't bound by tape.

Pulled slowly.

Watched a strand of the tape start to peel back, pulling bits of coloured paper into its sticky path.

I lifted the package up in front of my face and watched the socks fall to the table.

Somewhere in the room my brother laughed into his sleeve.

They were just like any pair she had made for me.

Made out of wool, these were the kind of socks that were perfect for a winter day from hell.

You know, when I'm out strutting through the Arctic like I have on so many occasions.

These were also blue, and although they were already folded together, I could still make out the white lightning-boltish design going up and down each sock.

I kept the grimace at bay and looked up to give my grandma the reaction she was waiting for.

"You've done it again, Grandma. Amazing job."

"I'm glad you like them. They're lucky socks, you know."

"Are they? How so?"

More muffled laughter from my brother.

"It's something you'll have to eventually find out for yourself," she said, looking a little too serious. "But turning twenty is a big step for a young man, and I thought you could use a little luck on your side."

"Grandma, no riddles. C'mon, just tell me!"

She laughed and took a small bite of cake off her plate.

"I'm afraid not, dear. You're going to have to find the luck yourself."

I groaned.

It was bad enough I spent my birthday, not out with friends, but with my entire bloodline, blowing out candles and wiping sauce off a kid's face.

Bad enough my night comes to an end with these foot warmers from hell in my face.

But now somebody thinks it's funny to invite the Riddler to my party.

Happy birthday to me.

* * *

I spent the next couple weeks enjoying all the winter options I had.

I played hockey with friends.

Built a giant snowman with my brother.

Which we then used as target practice with Roman candle fireworks.

I went tobogganing at night, drinking cheap beer in between slides to the bottom and the walk back up.

And the socks?

Well, they stayed buried at the bottom of my drawer with the rest of its unwanted brothers and sisters.

One day, after one such day of activities, I returned home, tired, sweaty and ready for a scalding shower and a cup of hot chocolate.

Walking into my room, I threw my parka, toque and gloves to the floor and grabbed a pair of sweat pants off my bed.

I turned around and made my way over to the dresser for a pair of boxers and socks.

The socks.

The "lucky" birthday socks, which had been sitting at the bottom of the unmentionables drawer, were now sitting atop my dresser, awaiting my hands to pluck them up from where they sat.

Frankie.

Frankie had come in while I was out and decided he had needed some more amusement at my expense.

But that couldn't be right.

Frankie had just left yesterday morning for a three-day snowboarding trip with some friends.

And I had been in my room many times since then.

Mom, perhaps?

Maybe trying to get a message across?

"Mom!"

No answer.

Damn it, that's right, she got called into work this morning.

And Dad had been at work before the sun even came up.

How the hell did they get here then?

Holding the socks out in front of me at arm's length, I ran to my closet and grabbed an old pair of worn out rollerblades off the top shelf.

"Let's see somebody find you now," I said, stuffing the socks into the one of the blades' boots.

And with that, they were out of sight, out of mind.

Now for that shower.

* * *

Just over a week later, I had decided to alter my schedule, waking with my father at five in the morning and, while he went to work, I would go to the gym.

I packed my gym bag with some shampoo and a change of clothes, grabbed my mother's cars keys and hit the road.

Just over a an hour later, drenched in sweat and in need of a swim in the gym's pool, I made my way down to the change room for my swim trunks and a towel.

I stopped dead in my tracks ten feet from my locker.

The socks.

The goddamn socks!

They were sitting on the bench that extended along every wall that held a locker.

Directly in front of mine.

Suddenly, the perspiration that had fired up my body felt ice cold, sending shivers down my spine every time the fabric rubbed against skin.

I told myself to relax, shaking off the ominous feeling that had sprouted from a pair of socks.

I walked over to the locker, keeping eyesight directly at the locker, as though the socks were staring up at me.

I pulled the lock attached to the door.

Still locked.

I quickly dialled in the combination, opened the door and seized my bag out and on to the bench.

I zipped it open and began ripping out every item I had placed inside.

Pants.

Sweater.

Shampoo.

Boxers.

Swim suit.

Towel.

Deodorant.

Hair gel.

And last but not least…a pair of white, cotton socks.

*Regular* white, cotton socks.

So how the hell did these get here?

I grabbed my birthday socks and held them in my hand.

Someone was playing a game.

But not a woohoo! fun kind of game.

It was like a I'm going to challenge myself at chess kind of game.

What was the angle?

Suddenly the socks began to feel warm as I moved them over in my hand, as though there were a foot inside them giving off heat.

I could feel the skin on my arms raise as a chill shot through my spine.

Get a hold of yourself, you pansy.

But I couldn't shake it.

I quickly made a decision.

Right then and there.

I shuffled over to the nearest garbage dispenser and, lifting the lid, tossed them into the dark abyss below.

And that was that.

Sorry Grandma.

* * *

That night I spent a lot of time making a groove in the couch, watching the Leafs game with my brother and father.

The boys in blue and white were playing the Sabres, and losing badly.

Seeing as it was the third period, I decided to skip the final buzzer and my brother's jeering (he was a Buffalo fan) and head up to my room to play some video games.

"Yeah I'd leave to if they were my team," Frankie said boldly to my retreating back.

I ignored him.

Somewhere upstairs, a toilet was calling for his toothbrush.

Passing through the dining room on my way up, I noticed my mother sitting at the table, reading one of her many horribly-written romantic novels.

"Mikey?" she said, her face still buried in the pages.

I stopped for a second, confused. That couldn't have been my mother talking to me. I could roll around on fire in front of her and she'd probably exit the room, annoyed I was making so much noise.

"Mom? Did you just say something?"

She put the book down, smiling at me.

"Yes, that was me. I wanted to ask you something."

"Sure."

"Have you talked to Grandma lately?"

I thought about it for a second before answering.

My grandmother usually called the house three times a week. Two out of three times she called to speak to me.

I hadn't spoken to her in two weeks. Not since my birthday.

"No," I said, genuinely concerned. "Do you think everything's alright?"

"Oh, she's fine. She's called here quite a few times actually. But she never asked for you."

I looked straight at her, feeling shocked a little bit hurt by this disclosure.

"Why doesn't she want to talk to me?"

My mother continued to stare at me, looking slightly perplexed.

"I don't know, Michael. I was hoping you could have told me."

"I have no idea? Should I call her?"

"I think you should. Tomorrow. See how she's doing and stuff. Sound good?"

"It does. Night, Mom."

"Goodnight, Mikey."

I hurried off upstairs, trying to ignore the feelings of hurt that stemmed from my grand-mommy not speaking to me.

Coming around the corner into my bedroom, I stopped dead in my tracks, almost swallowing my tongue in horror.

The socks were sitting in the middle of my bedroom floor.

I paused, unsure what to do or what to say.

What felt like an hour later, I grabbed the socks off the floor and stormed back downstairs.

I was going to stuff them in Frankie's mouth, make him choke on them for screwing with me.

This had never been funny to begin with.

Now it was borderline creepy.

I stopped on the bottom step.

Wait a minute, I thought. You can't do this. Not only are they going to think you've lost it, but you're going to flat out admit you tossed your dear old grandmother's present into the garbage can of a gym change room.

No.

I take care of this myself.

Thinking hard, I finally came to a miraculous realization.

Tomorrow was garbage day.

Tomorrow was victory.

* * *

I went down to breakfast the next morning feeling refreshed and happy.

Less than three hours ago, I had risen early to initiate mission Socks-Be-Gone.

I went downstairs before my father got up to gather the trash together.

Going into the kitchen, I drew the garbage pail from under the sink and buried the socks as far under as my hands could reach.

Then running back to bed, I listened for my father's footsteps and morning grumbles.

Ten minutes later, I watched from my window as he zombie walked his way to the end of the curb, garbage bag and recycling box in tow.

Not even fifteen minutes later, I heard the garbage truck pulling down our street.

Sitting from my window, I watched again as the truck pulled closer and closer to our house.

When he pulled up at the edge of our curb, I felt my heart pumping madly, my face pressed right into the glass in anticipation.

The guy got off the back of the truck.

Grabbed the garbage bag in his hands.

Walked to the back of the truck.

Lifted the bag over his head.

Heaved the bag into the truck.

Success!

And sitting here now, at the breakfast table, I bet you're wondering why I'm so happy.

Why I've gone to so much trouble to rid myself of a birthday gift.

A gift made out of love, from a grandmother to her grandson.

Well, I'll tell you.

It's the principle.

Somebody's playing games with me.

I don't play games.

I end them.

And hey, getting rid of a pair of useless socks at the same time ain't too shabby.

Two birds with one stone, right?

A thump came from the front door, interrupting my thoughts and morning cereal and toast.

"Michael!" my father's voice rang out from upstairs. "Can you get the paper please?"

Getting up from the table, I made my way to the door, half a piece of toast hanging from my mouth.

I opened the front door and felt the bread get stuck in my mouth.

Where the paper should have been, the socks were now sitting on the Welcome mat at my feet.

Choking and coughing back bits of toast, I looked around for whoever had thrown them at the front door.

Save for an elderly couple walking their dog on the other side of the street, there was no one around.

*This is impossible*, I thought. *What the hell is going on?*

I cautiously picked the socks off the ground.

This needs to end.

"Did you get the paper?" my father called.

I started to answer when a rolled up newspaper collided with the side of my head.

As the tiny lights stopped dancing around me, I turned and politely lifted my middle finger behind me.

Twelve-year-old laughter was the response.

"Yeah," I shouted back. "I got it!"

Paper and socks in each hand, I went inside and closed the door. This needs to end now.

* * *

That night I had an epiphany.

It was an epiphany of desperation, but an epiphany nonetheless.

I approached my mother with my plan.

"Mom? Can I ask you a favour?"

"Sure, honey."

"Can we donate some clothes?"

My mother looked at me curiously.

"Clothes? Really?"

"Yes. I was just going through my closet and everything and I really need to get rid of some clothes I don't wear anymore. Can we?"

"Umm...sure, yeah, I don't see why not," she replied. "Actually, if you can have everything ready by tomorrow morning, I'll drop everything off tomorrow afternoon."

"Excellent!" I said, clapping my hands together. "Thanks, Mom."

Just then the phone rang from the other room.

I ran to it and answered it before the third ring.

"Hello?"

A moment of silence.

"Michael?" the voice finally said.

'Grandma?"

"Hello, Michael."

"Hey Grandma! I've missed talking to you! How are things?"

"They're fine, Michael, thank you. Is your mother around?"

Something was off in her voice. I didn't like it.

"Yes, she is, but...Grandma, what's wrong? Did I do something to upset you?"

"What? Oh, no, sweetheart, just got a few things going through my head is all. Tell me, did you discover any luck with those socks yet?"

"Oh, well...not really. Been wearing them around," I lied. "So far nothing. But I'm not giving up!"

Silence on the other end.

"I see," she finally said. "Well, that's the important thing, Michael. Don't give up."

"Yes ma'am. But here's Mom. Talk to you soon Grandma!"

I handed the phone over to my mother and ran upstairs.

It was time to finish this thing.

\* \* \*

The following morning I had put together a box full of clothes, jackets, shoes and whatever else I could find.

Oh, and let's not forget a certain pesky pair of socks.

It's not like everything in the box was no longer desirable, or didn't fit.

But when you're going for a swim, you don't worry about getting your hair wet, do you?

I loaded the box into the back of my mother's car with the rest of what we were donating, and made sure to carefully check my box again.

The socks were still there, crushed under a slew of shirts, pants and old sandals.

Satisfied, I slammed the door shut and went back inside, whistling my own musical number.

I crossed my fingers two steps from my room, closed my eyes and stepped inside.

Inhaling deeply, I opened my left eye slightly and took a peek.

No socks.

Nothing dropping on my shoulder from the ceiling.

Nothing colliding with my head.

So far, as they say it, so good.

\* \* \*

It's been three days now.

I believe I've finally won this thing.

There's not been a sign or a sight of any socks but the ones I buy out of a package at the city's superstore.

See, those 'lucky' socks weren't the only ones I gave away that day.

No, Michael C. Mathers cleaned house that morning.

I'm twenty now.

Time to start acting like it.

And now, here I was, sipping hot chocolate from my favourite mug, stretched out on my dad's La-Z Boy chair with my feet up, watching the local news.

Life was good.

An insanely hot female reporter appeared on the screen, in front of what appeared to be a homeless shelter.

"It's a miraculous story, Jim. And for one local man, one that couldn't come a moment too soon."

I turned up the volume.

*Weird*, I thought.

*That looks like our city's homeless shelter.*

The woman continued.

"Almost a year ago today, thirty-nine year old Henry Kunitz was a family man. A business man. A happy man.

And then the unfortunate happened.

Henry was fired from his job. His wife of eighteen years took off with another man, Henry's three children in tow.

Less than two months later, Henry was evicted from his home, forcing him to live out of his truck for the next three months.

When money became almost non-existent, he sold his truck for a few hundred dollars, taking shelter wherever he could find it.

Spending the money at bars and racetracks, Henry eventually lost every cent.

The next day, he ended up here, on the doorstep of Helping Hands homeless shelter, where he's resided for the last six months."

The camera began to follow the reporter as she began moving to her left, stopping when she was next to a man.

Henry Kunitz, I'm assuming.

The man looked like he had hit rock bottom.

He was average height, slim build and pale.

He was carrying some heavy baggage under his eyes and his hair was dishevelled and unkempt.

But he looked genuinely happy about it.

"Helping Hands," the reporter continued, "has taken in those less fortunate for the last thirty years in this community.

They are a non-profit organization developed to give food, clothes and a warm bed to those who can't afford to do it themselves.

The only thing they've asked over the last three decades is that people of the community try and help any way they can, whether it's through volunteering or donating food, blankets or clothes."

She turned to the man next to her.

"Mr. Kunitz, would you mind telling us about the amazing day you've had?"

"Sure. Well...well...I've been in a real slump for a while. Everything that could've gone wrong for me, well...has. But today...today was a new day for me. A miracle."

Tears began to form at the corner of Henry Kunitz's eyes.

*Oh, brother*, I thought. *What happened? Did you find a half-eaten steak in the trash?*

Henry continued.

"I went down to the donation room, like I do every week, once a week. I really needed new socks and shoes, so..."

I sat up, eyes glued to the screen, inexplicably alert and focused.

"...through a few piles, when I came across a few socks made of wool. I asked if I could have them, and the nice ladies looking over everything said yes."

Henry then retrieved some of the socks from his coat pocket and held them up to the camera.

White socks with green stars.

Grey socks with red and white stripes.

Black socks with grey spots.

My socks.

Holy shit.

"I tried them all on. They fit perfectly, kept my foot warm, did their job, you know. And then I came upon the last pair I had just been given."

He held them up.

Blue socks. White lightning bolts in vertical lines.

I almost spit up my hot chocolate right then and there.

"Tell us, Mr. Kunitz," the reporter inquired, "what did you find when you put them on?"

Smiling widely with tears slipping down his face, Mr. Kunitz, hands shaking, removed a piece of paper from another pocket and held it up to the camera.

"I found this ticket."

I looked curiously at the wrinkled piece of paper in his hand.

*What the hell?*

"And not just any ticket, viewers," the reporter said excitedly. "But the four million dollar ticket from last month's LottoHaul!"

I felt my insides collapsing in shock.

Shivers came in waves, making my body twist and ripple in discomfort.

My brain felt as though static snowballs were being pelted around in my head.

*No, please, God, tell me I'm dreaming.*

"I never thought anything like this would ever happen to me," Henry Kunitz continued, sobbing into the camera. "Lucky socks, I tell you."

Funny, isn't it, the ironic cards fate plays you?

The very things I've grown to hate were used against me, bringing promises of bounty and reward to my feet, and I had been too ignorant to even try them on.

And no, I still don't give a rat's ass about who invented socks.

They're still not pretty to look at it.

They'll never look good in a pair of flip flops.

But I can already see my headstone years from now.

"O Lord, do I wish I had put them on."

If there's one thing I've learned about life, it's that fortune may knock on your door once or twice, but it's hard luck that knows how to endure.

*Dedicated to all grandparents,*

*And in loving memory of Elizabeth Rotella*

*Who always made sure that there was food in my belly, a dollar in my pocket and above all, that true warmth wasn't from the socks on your feet, but from the family you surrounded yourself with.*

*Love you Nana*

# Joey : Part 2

*By Chris*

I like my new home. My new Daddy and Mommy are both nice. The young boy's name is Timmy. There is a young girl too, her name is Julie.

I've been here for two years now. They love me here. They take care of me. Timmy and Julie play with me all the time. My new Mommy and Daddy take me for walks.

I still miss my old Mommy sometimes. I don't miss my old Daddy though. He's mean.

My new family takes me to see the man in the white coat sometimes too. I don't mind seeing him. I get special treats when we go there. I sit up on the table and I get a special treat while he pokes something sharp in my bum.

Timmy and Julie are gone a lot. They go to school. I always get excited and run to the door when I hear the bus dropping them off outside.

Mommy stays home all day though. When she does go out, she takes me in the car with her. I like the car. I like looking out the window at all the different things speeding by. Sometimes she lets me put my head out the window. That is fun too but it makes me really thirsty.

Daddy goes out most mornings and comes home later. He plays with me for a bit when he comes home. We go out in the back yard and he throws a ball for me to run after. It is so much fun. At dinner time Daddy always sneaks me food under the table and I like that too.

At night when Timmy goes to bed I go into his room. I have a bed in his room too. Mommy and Daddy tell me no when I try to sleep in Timmy's bed. After they close his door, Timmy always picks me up and brings me in bed with him. When Mommy or Daddy look in the room later and see me I get scared I will get in trouble but they only smile and put me back down in my own bed.

Nobody gets mad at me in my new house. They love me and I love them.

# Coffee or Tea

*By Tom*

He sat in the comfortably padded armchair of the Corner Street Café.

Seated in the outdoor patio, he sipped from a steaming cup as he watched the people around him.

He was an older man, somewhere in his sixties, with grey, thinning hair and a smooth, wrinkle-free face.

Although up in age, the heart of a young man seemed to beat inside.

His bright blue eyes were full of life, capable of expressing multiple emotions in chorus.

A faint breeze disrupted the otherwise calm and silence of the autumn air, catching the hairs under the man's nose.

He lifted his arm under his nose and lightly sneezed into the fabric of his egg white, v-neck sweater.

"God bless you, old friend."

The man didn't turn at the voice behind him, but continued to stare around, his lips stretching into a smile.

"I was beginning to wonder when you'd arrive, Lucius," he replied softly, getting to his feet to face his friend.

The man before him was younger, probably in his late twenties.

He had the look of an up and coming actor in Hollywood: perfect tan, perfect teeth perfect hair and a physique to match.

He wore dark, fitted blue jeans and a black polo with a red collar.

His black hair was short and looked like it had taken a hairdryer, four mirrors and half a container of mousse to style it.

Tinted aviator sunglasses covered his eyes, and, like the old man, Lucius also wore a smile.

However, whereas his elder's smile seemed to radiate with love and energy and joy, the younger man's smile seemed blank and emotionless.

"You have quite a taste in location, Emmanuel," Lucius said, extending his hand.

"It's such a perfect day out," the old man replied happily, holding out his own hand. "Fall is perhaps my favourite season."

They shook hands and sat down opposite of one another.

"I see not much changes with you," Lucius said, shaking his head as he observed the old man's appearance. "Always the old school look."

"Nor with you," Emmanuel replied. "Such a constant need to draw attention to yourself."

Lucius laughed, still wearing a smile devoid of happiness.

"It's so rare I get to leave the office," he said, running a hand through his perfect hair. "The opportunity is just too tempting to pass up."

Just then, a waitress, young, blonde and smiling wide enough to glimpse every pearly white within her mouth, approached the table.

"Hello there," she said flirtatiously, eyes locked on Lucius, obviously entranced by his appearance. "Can I get you anything?"

"Forgive me," Emmanuel said to the young man, pointing to his still steaming cup. "I wasn't sure when you would arrive."

"Not at all," Lucius replied, holding up his own hand, looking up at the waitress. "Can I trouble you for a coffee, my dear? Black?"

"Of course, honey," she responded, batting her eyelashes. "My name's Ashley. Be back in a minute."

The two sat quietly a moment after the young lady had rushed off.

"You're silent, old man," Lucius said suddenly. "Could it be disgust that holds your tongue?"

The old man looked genuinely stumped by the question.

"I'm afraid I don't understand the question, my friend," he replied calmly.

"Oh come now, Emmanuel," the young man retorted. "Don't play the blind fool. We both saw the darkness lurking inside of her. Admit it."

The old man glanced over at the young waitress as she made her way back to the table, her eyes fixated directly at the young heartthrob seated across from him.

"Here's your coffee, hun," she said, lowering the mug in front of Lucius. "Careful now, it's extremely hot."

"The only way to drink it," he replied, flashing a perfect smile at her. "Wouldn't you agree, beautiful?"

The woman blushed furiously at his address to her, and seemed to lose her composure for a second.

"Y-Yes," she stammered finally, looking over quickly at the older man. "Can I get you a refill on your tea, sir?"

"No, my dear," he replied, smiling at her. "I am more than content at the moment, thank you."

"Yes, Ashley," Lucius said smoothly. "You've been absolutely to die for."

Reaching out, he gently took the young woman's hand in his.

Within seconds, the woman's smile vanished.

Her mouth was closed tight, lips pulled in as though she had just tasted a freshly cut lemon or lime.

Her eyes were open wide, bulging in some unseen terror or pain.

"Lucius!"

Emmanuel's voice was soft but rang out with authority.

Lucius scowled, but let go of the young lady's hand.

She blinked once and seemed to instantly forget what had just happened.

"OK," she said cheerfully, "I'll be back in a bit to check up on you boys."

Allowing herself another playful look at Lucius, she walked off to her next table.

"That was unwise, my friend."

Lucius smiled, ignoring the reprimand.

"The slut deserved it," he spat. "Tell me she didn't."

"We are here for one reason today. Interfering with other matters we will not."

"Oh please," the young man said, shaking with anger. "Whores, liars and thieves. All of them sinners. You saw the lust and desire clouding her heart. The things she wanted to do to me. The hunger that she craved to satisfy. Would you call me a liar?"

The old man stared at him.

"No, I will not, old friend. But we both agree our history seems to sit on opposite sides of the coin."

Smiling, Lucius took a long sip of the hot, steaming coffee and placed the empty cup back on the table.

"Ah yes. How soon I forget. The creator. The forgiver. The eternal believer in good overcoming evil."

"We have had these arguments before, my friend…"

"And to what avail?" Lucius said. "What has been solved, other than you overruling anything I've said?"

"Lucius…,"

"You say we are all entitled to our own choices!" the young man continued. "But what of my choices? Why are my choices so wrong? Why do you look down on me? Because I chose to be a god, and not a servant of one?"

Emmanuel sat up straight in his chair and cleared his throat.

"You're right," he said calmly. "I do allow free will. And I have always given you the right to choose which path that freedom wills you to take. I do not look down upon you, old friend. But I am the one who has walked and battled through the elements to create those paths, and I will not let another's choices lay ruin to them."

Lucius said nothing, but seemed to burn with an unspoken rage.

"And man?" he finally said, with a hint of sarcasm. "You allow man the freedom to walk and roam wherever they choose, when they have proved they would fair better at the end of a tight leash."

And that is where we differ, old friend," Emmanuel replied softly. "You are convinced that they are all hopelessly lost, when I have seen for myself the places they have actually gone."

"You made a mistake giving them free will."

"Should they not be allowed to live and learn for themselves?" the old man countered, his eyes blazing with a gentle fire. "Good and evil. Love and hate. Coffee or tea," he added, pointing to each of their cups. "It is our choices, and we must live with them. I have faith that they will learn. Tomorrow is another day, my friend."

"Ha!" Lucius sneered. "I remember the last time you spoke those words. The last time you put your faith so heavily in man and the right thing. Do you remember what tomorrow brought, Emmanuel? What was it called? World War Two?"

Emmanuel sighed heavily,shaking his head.

"You are so full of hatred, brother."

Lucius smiled wide, revealing the teeth within, each one coming to a sharp and pointed tip.

"Hate is what drives me," he said. "Hatred allows me to see what your pathetic love and faith can not. There is no camaraderie between men. I have seen the damage and pain they're capable of. They will tear out one another's hearts for something as simple as a parking spot during the Christmas holidays."

"Enough!" Emmanuel shouted, slamming his fist down on the table. The lights in the coffee shop suddenly flickered, all eyes on the two men arguing.

Emmanuel smiled and closed his eyes. A moment later, everyone around them returned to what they had been doing, oblivious that there had ever been an interruption.

"Old age," Lucius said, clearly enjoying himself, "is a terrible thing."

"It is not that," Emmanuel replied, once again totally calm. "Our guest has arrived."

The two looked to the front entrance.

Standing there, looking terrified and confused, was a man.

He was middle aged, garbed in an oversized blue-hooded sweater, matched with a pair of black tearaway track pants.

He had a few days growth spread around his neck and face, his hair was matted and dishevelled, and there were dark marks under his eyes.

Emmanuel rose to his feet, smiling wide, eyes sparkling bright, arms open, beckoning to this new face.

Lucius continued to sit, still at a statue, the dark sunglasses concealing the true monster within.

Upon seeing Emmanuel gesturing to him, he slowly and awkwardly made his way over to their table.

"Jeffrey!" the old man exclaimed, pulling up a third chair to the table. "My dear boy, sit sit!"

The man hesitated, staring between the two men staring at him.

"Do I know you?"

"Sit when you're told to sit, boy," Lucius growled, still rooted in the chair.

Jeffrey stared down at the young man before him.

"Who the hell are you?" he asked angrily, eyebrows raised. "Who the hell are either of you? How did I get here?"

Emmanuel smiled.

"All questions will be answered, Jeffrey, in due time. Let's sit and talk."

After a few moments, their guest slowly seated himself between the two strangers.

"It's Jeff," he said. "Just call me Jeff."

"Jeffrey Ladd, Jr.? Is that not your given name?" the old man asked.

"It was my father's name," the man replied bitterly. "I haven't gone by that name since I was twelve. How did you know that? How do you know me?"

"We know everything about your pathetic excuse for a life," Lucius muttered nastily.

"Lucius!" The old man exclaimed harshly. "Remember why we are here."

The young man smiled unpleasantly.

"Of course," Lucius said his hand rising towards his face. "Where are my manners?"

As his fingers grasped the frame of the glasses, he pulled the aviators down his nose and off his face.

As he looked up, Jeff recoiled in horror.

Something was lurking beneath the surface of the young man's eyes. Something evil.

The pupils, blacker than a starless night, seemed cold and barren yet capable of burning straight through anything they gazed upon.

As Jeff sat, hypnotized by the worms and spiders that seemed to wriggle within Lucius' eyes, he had a sudden feeling of sickness and despair, as though the man had reached into Jeff's insides and taken a stranglehold on his soul.

"What do you say, Jeff?" Lucius said softly, watching Jeff tremble in his gaze. "Shall we talk?"

Looking straight down at the table, Jeff muttered "OK."

"Excellent!" Emmanuel exclaimed, clapping his hands together. "Ask your questions, dear boy! Ask away!"

Jeff looked up, staring at the old man smiling back at him.

"Who are you guys? What am I doing here?"

"I believe in order to answer your first question," Emmanuel replied, eyes twinkling, "we need to answer the second."

"Do you know where you were before you arrived at the coffee shop?"

Jeff sat there, total confusion etched into his features, as he attempted to recall something.

"I'm not sure," he said, rubbing his temples. "I remember… I remember loud sounds…"

The two other men stared at him, silent, offering him no assistance or encouragement.

Suddenly, a bolt of lightning seemed to touch down in Jeff's mind, opening up lost memories and images.

Desert.

Sun.

Overwhelming heat.

Never-ending stretches of road.

Shouting.

Gunfire.

Explosions.

Death.

"I was a soldier," he said softly.

More pictures and scenes began racing through his mind, and he grabbed the sides of his head as if in pain.

"I remember it all," he cried out, rocking back and forth. "Make it stop."

"Tell us," Emmanuel urged him, resting his hand on Jeff's arm.

Jeff stopped rocking and slowly removed his hands from his face.

"I was on duty in Afghanistan," he continued, mouth twitching. "And I died."

The two men sitting on either side of him suddenly moved closer, the legs of the chairs gliding noiselessly against the concrete floors.

"So if I'm dead… that means… you two are…"

The two men did not respond, but continued to stare at him.

"No. It can't be…"

"It can't?" Lucius responded, eyebrows raised. "Well please, do tell us what it is then."

Jeff swallowed hard. As he looked around at the people in the coffee shop, he caught sight of his reflection in the patio's glass doors.

His entire appearance had changed, all the way to the clothes he had died in.

He was dressed in tan, grey and green camouflage gear.

And where his hair was long and unkempt, a combat helmet was now perched atop his shaved head.

He stared at his reflection, mesmerized by the change that had taken place.

"I don't believe it," he managed to say.

"Not our problem," Lucius snapped. Turning to Emmanuel, he asked, "Shall we move on?"

The old man nodded, eyes still focused on Jeff.

"Perfect!" Lucius exclaimed, clapping his hands together happily. "So…Jeffrey. What shall we do with you, hmm"?

Jeff suddenly looked frightened.

"Do with me?"

Lucius smiled in response.

"What my friend means," Emmanuel responded, casting Lucius a disapproving look, "is that everything has its season. Wouldn't you agree, Jeffrey?"

Jeff made no sound, subdued by the way this old man seemed to communicate as though they were in a classroom.

Instead he just nodded.

The old man watched as a maple leaf, separated from the branch of its tree, fluttered in the wind, straight into his outstretched hand.

"And just as in your case," he said, twirling the leaf gently between his fingers, "we must wait and see what the new season will bring."

Jeff sat there, his mind still unable to turn thoughts into words.

Instead he nodded again.

"So," Emmanuel began, "there are particular questions we need to ask you in order to, if I may say so, determine your forecast?"

Jeff nodded again, head drooped.

"I would like to begin," the old man continued, gazing sternly "with Joni."

Jeff's head snapped up, eyes blazing.

"How dare you…"

"Watch your tone, boy," Lucius growled.

Jeff looked between the two of them, before slumping in defeat.

Emmanuel's gaze softened.

"You loved your wife, Jeffrey?"

"More than anything."

"You would have done anything for her?"

"Anything. Everything," he cried, rubbing his eyes.

"And what happened to her, Jeffrey?"

Jeff stared back at both men, lips pressed together, eyes full of venom.

"*God* took her from me."

"Ha!" Lucius exclaimed, pointing at Jeff. "Do you see, old man? They want and need things their own pathetic lives desire but cannot attain. They pray for miracles and answers to life's little problems. But when God doesn't provide? They curse your name and cast you out of their lives!"

"That will do, Lucius."

Turning to Jeff, Emmanuel spoke in almost a whisper.

"Your wife did not blame God when she became ill, Jeffrey."

"No, but..."

"And she did not curse the Heavens when it became clear that things were not going to get better."

"No, but..."

"And instead of seeing the true beauty in front of you, you chose to look at your life through a broken mirror."

"True beauty?" Jeff asked, his eyes full of tears.

"What happened to your wife was tragic, Jeffrey. She was young. Beautiful. Caring. So full of life. So much to give to the world. But those characteristics were not God's doing. They were hers. She was brought into this world, just as any, to walk her own path. And every choice she made led straight to you."

Jeff did not answer, but sobbed into his hands.

"True love is such a complicated part of life," Emmanuel continued, his eyes also brimming with tears. "Begins with a look, a smile. Grows with each hug, kiss and embrace.

He touched Jeff's arm, grasping it firmly.

"And the truest love always ends in teardrops."

Jeff looked up at the old man, sadness spilling over in every valley of his heart.

"I was so lost after she died."

Emmanuel nodded sympathetically, but it was Lucius who spoke up.

"And how did you repay that love, dear Jeffrey?"

Jeff did not answer, but continued to sob.

"I will tell you," Lucius continued, smiling widely. "You drank. You smoked. You quit your job. You cut yourself off from your family and friends. You sold your wedding ring just to keep the bottles in your hand."

Jeff nodded half heartedly, his eyes red and swollen.

"And three years later, when the pain wouldn't go away, you joined the army didn't you? Thought it take your mind off of her?"

Again Jeff nodded, grief consuming his ability to speak.

"What happened in Afghanistan, Jeffrey?"

"Please," Jeff pleaded, "please stop."

"Tell us what happened," Lucius ordered.

Eyes facing the tiles of the floor, Jeff cleared his throat.

"We were in a small village. Shots were being fired at us. Our squad took cover where we could find it. Some of us fired back, created a diversion. The rest of us went in, staying in the shadows. I...I..."

"Keep going," Lucius sneered.

"We split up. I went in through an abandoned house. I h-heard a sound. Someone coming down the stairs. I hid on the other side of the wall. Saw their shadow. Getting closer. Came around the corner. I fired...," he whimpered.

Lucius grinned at the weeping man before him, his teeth bared menacingly.

"And what did you find, Jeffrey?"

"It was...was...a boy!" he howled. "Six. Maybe seven. I killed a boy!"

"Finish!" Lucius screamed.

"We left. K-kept going. I went ahead. I couldn't...couldn't think straight. They shouted at me. Told me to stop. Warned me. I kept going. And then...and then..."

"And then you died," Lucius said. "A land mine?"

Jeff nodded, his face racked with guilt.

"Such a disappointment," Lucius sighed, staring over at the old man. "I've made my decision."

"I'm sure you have," Emmanuel responded, eyes on Jeff. "But our meeting is not over just yet, old friend."

Lucius stared open-mouthed back, loathing all over his face.

"You can't be serious? This man's life is worth nothing! He blames God for the man he is today! He killed a child! He attempted to destroy himself through self abuse and deliberate endangerment! And in doing so he destroyed the memory of someone who truly loved him! What is there to be salvaged by showing him salvation?"

Emmanuel paused a moment before answering.

"His soul."

Lucius stared, dumbfounded.

"You're a fool," he said softly.

Emmanuel rose from his chair, towering over the two other men.

Jeff sat in silent awe as he watched the power and command that seemed to emanate from the old man.

"Snake," he hissed, pointing a finger at Lucius, who withdrew farther into his chair. "You have always been blind of man's potential. You would rather watch a man burn for his sins rather than look into his heart for truth."

"You would argue against me then?" Lucius growled, teeth bared.

"I would. This man's something became nothing only when his love was taken from him. He lives every second with guilt for being the one who has had to survive all this time. And all this pain because she was the only person whom he truly loved. I believe it is now his choice which path he takes."

Lucius shrieked in frustration, and leaned in towards Jeff.

"Come now, boy," he whispered into the man's ear. "Think about it. Riches. Women. All the guilt washed away and every deepest desire fulfilled. All for one little nod of the head, what do you say? Just tell me what you want."

Jeff did nothing for a moment, but stared into his hands. A few seconds passed by, when suddenly, he rose to his feet.

"I want to hold Joni in my arms again."

Lucius roared with fury and rose to his feet.

"You fools," he spat. "You can not erase the doings of his past. Can't ignore the the things he's done."

Emmanuel stepped forward, placing an arm around Jeff's shoulders.

"It is true," he said kindly, "that I cannot do. He will never be able to go back and start over. But from this moment, he can create a new ending."

Lucius spat at their feet and began to walk through the patio, back inside and over to the entrance door of the café, the people around them oblivious to it all.

"Man is the punch line to a dreadful joke," he shouted, his back to them. "Let's hope one day you open your eyes."

And with that, he walked out into the street and disappeared.

A silence there, between Jeff and the old man, until Jeff could no longer stand it.

"So what happens now?"

Emmanuel looked over, smiling wide and eyes twinkling.

"Now?" he asked cheerfully. "Well, I suppose I will quickly finish my tea and we will be off. Your wife is waiting for you."

Jeff smiled, feeling happiness that he had not felt in years.

He was going home.

# The Job

*By Chris*

Clint had to prepare. They were coming soon but he had time. He had to get everything ready. He enjoyed the evening air as he walked out to his garage. As he walked, he pulled his keys from his pocket, putting his index finger through the ring and spinning them around as he made his way across the gravel driveway.

When he got to the door, he found the key he needed. The padlock opened with ease. He undid the latch, opened the door and flipped the switch. One thousand watts of light flickered and struggled to illuminate the dark room. With the shadows disappearing he walked in and shut the door.

He got a call from Lance about an hour ago saying that they had just killed her. They were supposed to kill her yesterday but were delayed. Lance had called to see if Clint was available for the job. Clint had made sure to be available. This is what he loved to do.

Clint turned on the small radio he kept in the garage for when he worked. AC/DC was just finishing up as U2's Sunday bloody Sunday faded in. He liked retreating and working out here, in the house Emilia wouldn't let him listen to this kind of music. Out here, this was his domain. She rarely came out here, and when she did, she didn't enter the building. She always talked to him from the doorway.

She had only come inside the building once while he was working. At the moment she entered he had just finished cutting off a foot. He wasn't sure if it was the blood or just the thought of him holding a severed body part but whatever it was, it was enough to cause her stomach to empty all over the floor.

Remembering it now, he could only laugh about it.

He stood at the foot of the table. It was made of stainless steel, eight feet long and three feet wide. It had a four inch lip around the entire perimeter and a trough leading to a hole at one end. The table sat at an almost imperceptible angle so as to lead the fluids down to the end with the hole so they could be easily washed away into a bucket underneath.

Even with the table being able to drain itself he still liked to take extra care keeping things clean. He walked over to a cabinet in the far wall. Grasping the brass handle he opened the door to reveal rolls of plastic laying down inside. He grabbed the closest roll and made his way back to the table, grabbing his scissors from a drawer as he passed by. Clint laid the plastic across the table neatly, letting it overhang evenly on both sides. He cut the roll and returned the plastic and scissors neatly to their homes.

There was a rolling table against the wall near the cabinet with the plastic. The table was stainless steel and covered with a white cloth. Clint removed the cloth to reveal a row of very sharp knives and saw-like instruments. He carefully folded the cloth and laid it on the counter. Looking down at the knives, a smile came across his face. The care he showed for them was close to that which he showed his wife. He spent more time holding and tending to these stainless steel instruments than he did to her. He loved Emelia, he truly did, but in here, he felt at home, at peace. He felt like a king.

Clint rolled the cart over next to the table. Using his foot, he carefully locked all the wheels so the cart would not roll away on him. Picking up the largest knife, he laid it on the plastic.

Now to wait.

It was only five or so minutes before he heard the truck pull up outside the garage. Clint walked over, and pulled up the rolling door. Two men jumped out of the truck and walked around to the back. Clint walked over to the table and waited. The two men were struggling as they entered the garage. One man had her by the hips, while the other held her shoulders. She was big. Her bare pink flesh rippled with every step the men took. With Clint's help they managed to get her up onto the table and onto her back..

Clint walked the two men out, then rolled the door back down upon their exit. He turned around and walked back towards the table, taking in the sight of her. The shape of her legs, the roundness of her belly, her protruding nipples, her thick neck. Clint walked over to the cupboard, opened it, and pulled a box of latex gloves out and placed them on the counter. Taking two from the box, he pulled them on as he made his way over to the table.

He picked up the knife, admiring how it glinted in the light, and set to work. He jabbed the knife into her belly and began to cut upwards, towards her neck. He made it through the belly just fine but when he got to the ribs, he had to grab one of the bone saws from the cart. Using that, he managed to get through her chest and up to her neck.

Placing the utensils down, he walked over and grabbed the garbage can next to the counter and brought it over to the table. He placed it down, then opened up the incision he made. Using the knife again, he began to cut out her organs and intestines and everything else. When he was satisfied she was empty, he grabbed a towel from under the table and dried her insides the best he could.

Throwing the towel into the garbage, he now grabbed a face shield from a hook on the wall. Putting it on, he grabbed a cleaver from the cart and made his way to the end of the table.

He grabbed her chin and raised her head. He raised the cleaver up, and brought it down on her thick neck. It took him four whacks to get through while being splattered with blood and fragments of bone.
After getting her head separated, he picked it up and tossed it into the trashcan. Clint walked back and placed the cleaver back onto the cart.

Picking the large knife back up again he began to separate one of her legs from her body. He was able to do it with speed and precision due to the number of times he had done it over the years. Next he made his way to the other end of her body and did the same thing with her shoulders.

Having those parts separated he was able to flip over her body with relative ease. Clint then picked up the bone saw again, and began to saw alongside her spine. He finished with one side then moved on and did the other. When he was done, he tossed her spine into the trash as well. Looking at the table, he now had her separated into six parts. Each part being a manageable size. Piece by piece, he picked her up and put her into a large cooler at the back of the room. She would stay well enough in there until she was picked up in the morning.

He folded up the bloody plastic from the table and stuffed it into the trash bag along with her spine, entrails and head. Clint tied the bag shut and pulled the can back over to the wall. He wheeled the cart over to the counter at the back of the garage and placed them in the sink where he began to quickly but meticulously clean them.

That being done he took a bucket of soapy water and a cloth over to the table and cleaned until it too was spotless.

Pulling a hose out from under the sink, he hooked it up to the tap. Turning on the hot water, he began to hose down the floor of the garage, letting the blood, skin and bone fragments flow towards the two drains he had in the floor.

When he was finished he picked up the phone and dialed Lance. After a few rings he picked up.

"Hey Lance, it's Clint."

A pause while Lance talked.

"I'm good, I'm good. Just wanted to let you know that she has been taken care of."

Another pause.

"Yes, you can pick her up in the morning."

Something Lance said made Clint laugh. Then another pause.

"Yes sir, the usual, hocks, loins and ribs."

Another pause.

"No sir, I didn't pickle the feet, they are still attached."

A pause.

"What's that sir, you want some cut up into bacon?"

Pause.

"I don't want any sir, we don't eat pork. But thank you anyway."

Clint hung up the phone.

# Airplanes

*By Chris*

It's been seven years since the day that the bombs were dropped. The first day of the end of the world as we knew it, and I remember it like it was yesterday.

The world had been in turmoil for close to a year with almost every single country at war with someone. Every night the news was full of reports outlining bombings and attacks and such. Death tolls were high, with thousands dying worldwide on a daily basis. People were frightened all over but life had to continue as well. People still had to work, children still had school, and life went on as normally as it could. You just had to wish that it wasn't your office building or your child's school getting hit by a car bomb or some other kind of terrorist act.

I remember it was a Friday. I had come home from work and was watching the news over dinner when it suddenly broke that North Korea had announced that they were launching a nuke against us.

Against us.

The U.S. of A.

How fucking dare they?

They claimed that they had captured a squad of American soldiers running black-ops in the country and were considering it an act of terrorism. The president denied it. No surprise there, but it seemed the North Koreans had had enough of being bullied and were launching at eight o'clock, Eastern Standard Time. I was in a daze. Here I am watching the six o'clock news, eating dinner, and in two hours I'd have a nuke dropping on my head.

Shit.

I continued watching to see if maybe, just maybe this was some kind of practical joke but it wasn't. The president came on and basically stated that he wasn't going to take that shit lying down and launched two nukes right back in the other direction.

After we launched, it seemed like everybody started getting in on the action. I think any and every country that had nuclear weapons decided to launch them against someone else. I don't even think at the time that the politicians in charge even cared who they were aiming at, as long as they were aiming at someone.

Panic ensued. People flooded the streets with their cars, motorcycles, bicycles, anything that would get them away faster. Trying to get somewhere, anywhere. The news had said there were places to go and be safe. They said some of the mountains in Pennsylvania had been hollowed out and underground cities had been built inside. These cities were supposedly fully stocked with years worth of food and water and other supplies. Foolishly half of America believed it and they all went straight for it.

Never believe half the stuff you see on T.V. All that talk about places to be safe was nothing but pipe dreams and bullshit. Panic spread across the globe in the hours between first launch and first detonation. People running, screaming, even killing each other to get what or where they wanted. Most of them, believing that there were safe havens, traveled hours only to be let down, or shot down.

I was one of the lucky ones. There was an old bomb shelter built in to the ground on my property. The door to which was in my basement. In the two years leading up to the first launch, as tensions were getting high across the planet, I had begun to stock the shelter up. I also modified it when it became clear that nuclear war might actually become a reality. In the end, about a month before the bombs came, I had changed it from a one room bunker into what was basically an underground, airtight two bedroom apartment.

Not only were there two bedrooms but there was also a small living area with an old couch and a battery operated radio. There was a storeroom down there as well. In it was a generator with barrels of fuel and it was also fully stocked with enough supplies to sustain four people for four years if my math was correct. There was what was basically an outhouse down there as well, it had taken a long time to dig the pit underneath it, I only hoped it was deep enough if the time ever came to use it.

There was one more room. It measured eight by eight. It was small, but it only had one use. Instead of a concrete floor, that one had been left as dirt. Three holes had been dug into the floor with all the excess dirt piled off to the side. I don't need to tell you what that room was for now do I?

The filtration system for the air was one of those FilteRite systems. We've all seen the commercials. "Guaranteed to give you clean air, even in the event of nuclear winter." I'm still here so it must have worked.

My buddy Ron lived across the street from me. He was always making fun of me, calling me paranoid. We had grown up together and usually he was the one being picked on. He had been overweight his entire life. Now, at thirty years old he was easily pushing three hundred pounds. When he found out about the bombs, he immediately came to me begging to let him and his family come into my shelter with me.

Now let me explain something, as far as people go, Ron and his wife Judy were nice enough, but I had my doubts about letting them in with me because frankly, they were two fat, lazy fucks. Back in school I had had a crush on Judy. Back in the day she was one of the prettiest girls in school. I don't know how Ron ended up with her. I had a feeling it was because he came from money. They had a child together and ever since the pregnancy she had packed on the pounds as well.

I was worried that they would use up all the supplies long before the four years was up. I needed the supplies to last that long because that was how long the scientists predicted it would take for the air on the surface to be breathable again.

In the end I let them come with me simply because I think I really just didn't want to be alone for that long. Ron assured me that him and Judy would stick to the ration schedule so that the supplies would last as long as they were supposed to. They packed up what they thought they needed from their home and stuffed it all into what would be their room in the shelter.

When we finally all crammed in, I found that it was a lot tighter than I anticipated. When we were all out in the main room, it was crowded. I know I said I had four years and four people's worth of supplies but originally it was only supposed to be two.

Me and Anna.

Anna was the love of my life. We had been together for twelve years before this whole thing started. When I was finally finished modifying and supplying the shelter, we got into an argument about how crazy I was spending so much money supplying something that I would never in my lifetime use. And how she could never be locked underground for four years. I tried to tell her that the only alternative to being underground in a shelter was being underground in a fucking coffin, but she just didn't get it.

One day when I had come back from getting supplies, I found a note on the table. Basically she had written that she thought I was a nut and she couldn't take being with me anymore. As I sit here now the only thing I can think is, How do you like me now bitch?

I turned on the FilteRite system and after a moment the air took on almost a sour flavor. After a few minutes of breathing it though, our bodies seemed to get used to it. I helped them situate themselves inside. Putting their things away and stuff like that.

That first night was deathly quiet. I laid in my bed and thought that this must be what it's like to be dead. Except for my breathing, the silence was total.

Hours ago we had heard noise from up top. It had sounded like a freight train was running right across the roof of the shelter. The ground shook as the blast wave went over top of us, presumably destroying everything in its path. Those first moments after the blast were the scariest as we waited to see if we would choke to death on the radiation or if the FilteRite system would actually work as it was supposed to.

Right after the blast, the air took on the smell of something burning and became so hot that it had seemed like our lungs would be scorched from the heat, but that only lasted a minute or so, then it went back to normal. At that time it was so far so good.

The first six months or so went by pretty routinely. Every day I would hand out everyone's rations. I was the only one with a key to the storage room, so they only got to eat what I gave them. Sometimes they would complain they were still hungry but then I would remind them that we were here for four years and had to make the food last. I think they still cursed me from their bedroom but I really didn't care. I had a plan and I was sticking to it.

After handing out the food, I would then go to the radio and systematically check the entire AM and FM dials for a signal. I don't think I ever actually expected to get a signal, after all we were underground. Finding no signal I would then take an inventory of everything from the food to the batteries. I would mark off the day on the calendar, check the clocks, then go and read a book.

I had lamps in each room running off the battery-generator system I had hooked up. I would run the generator long enough to charge the batteries then shut it off. During the day when we were all in the living area we only needed the one lamp in there. At night when we were in separate rooms the batteries would be charged and we would all use our own lamps. When they died out, it was time to sleep.

Things were actually looking good for Ron and Judy. They were steadily losing weight, I think because the rations were small. After six months it looked like Ron was down to two fifty and Judy had dropped to what looked like around one eighty. Their kid Johnny was doing good too. He was a good shit, didn't whine too much. Sometimes during the day I would sit with him and color, or read, or just play with him.

One problem I had was on the nights when Johnny was asleep and they decided to have sex. Now don't get me wrong, it's o.k. that they did, after all, it's human nature. Some nights I would lay in my own bed listening to them and jerk myself off. I loved listening to the sounds she would make. Sometimes while I was doing it I would think of Anna or picture Judy back in high school and those were the times I would orgasm so hard it seemed like it would never end. Other times while stroking it, a mental picture of Ron and Judy as fat slobs would come to mind, and those times I would struggle to finish because my dick would go limp and it would be like playing with a wet spaghetti noodle, if I could even finish at all.

All that aside, I did actually find their company enjoyable. I don't know if it is because it was the only company that I had or if I actually did like them more than I thought. Some days we would play cards and other days just sit and talk. At first we would talk a lot about the past, but as time wore on we found ourselves talking more and more about the future.

What was it going to be like when we finally opened the doors? Were we going to find a world totally devoid of life? Were we going to find new life forms? What about other people? How many others were surviving across the world in shelters like the one we were in? We would mull these questions over with each other for hours on end night after night until we were about two years in and one day Johnny came up with the stumper of stumpers.

What if we can't even get the door open?

That question had never even entered my mind before. Since the door to this shelter was in the basement of my home, what if my home collapsed in front of the door? I thought about that question for days, it even kept me up nights as well. I was tempted to try the door now, two years early, just to see if the door would move. I knew that if I did try it though that everything I had done to survive would be for nothing. We would have to wait and just hope that when the time came, the door would open and the way would be clear for us to venture out into the world.

At around the two and a half year mark, things began to change. Better or worse? Who's to say, but I'll explain it all to you now and let you be the judge.

I don't know how it happened but I had suddenly begun to find myself attracted to Judy. Maybe I was tired of my masturbatory fantasies or maybe it was the fact that she was becoming an attractive woman again. I tend to think that it was because she was the only woman around. She had gotten down to about one hundred and fifty pounds and was returning to her former beauty. That is not skinny by most men's standards but if they had seen her when she first came in here they would agree that she was much more beautiful now. Also take into account that because of the dramatic weight loss, Ron and Judy were both dressing minimally due to the fact that their clothes just didn't fit anymore. They asked me if it was o.k. if they dressed down and I told them that as long as it didn't bother them I would be fine with it.

One day I came out of my room and Judy was cleaning up the toys laying around after Johnny went to bed. I was going to the food closet to get everyone their evening water ration. When I came out I asked Judy where Ron was and she told me he had a headache and had already gone to bed for the night. I handed her the bottles of water for her and her family. She set them on the table and returned to cleaning up the toys. I don't know what came over me, but she was wearing just her bra and panties and when she had set the bottles down, the way she moved had caused a stirring in my shorts. Watching her on her hands and knees, cleaning the toys was just more than I could take.

I set my bottle down on the table and then I walked over to where I was standing behind her. I watched her for what seemed like an hour but in reality was probably only two seconds. I bent over and put both of my hands on her hips. Without looking she stopped what she was doing and just stayed in place, allowing me to feel her bare skin. I moved my hands down her hips and then down her thighs, pulling her panties down with one movement. I was hard now and pulled my shorts down. She still never looked back, she only whispered the words "Do it.". When I entered her it felt incredible. I don't know whether she felt that good or it had just been too long but after only three thrusts I was finished.

Suddenly guilt overtook me and I hurriedly stood up, pulling up my shorts in the process. I grabbed my bottle of water from the table and hurried back to my room and shut the door. While I was laying there that night I couldn't get the image of her down on all fours out of my head.

The next couple days passed with me staying in my room as much as I could. I guess I was trying to avoid them so as not to give Ron any indication that anything had happened. About a week later I came out one morning to find her alone sitting at the table. She smiled at me and it was then that I realized she really was a beautiful woman. "I didn't tell him." She said to me. I told her that was good and I was sorry and that it wouldn't happen again. "Why not?" She asked me. I was at a loss for words and the only thing I could come up with was the fact that she was married.

She stood and walked over to me. She grabbed my hand and put it up to her breast. "Any time you want me."

Again I was at a loss for words.

I turned away to go to the food closet and it was just in time, as her bedroom door opened and out came Ron. After a few minutes I handed out the rations and retreated back to my room.

Everything stayed quiet for a couple months. I was still doing my daily routines. They were still doing their daily things. Then one day about three years in Johnny was sick in bed burning up with a fever. Ron and Judy panicked as we took an inventory of the medicines I had stockpiled. There really wasn't much. Other than Aspirin and Advil there were mostly only cough medicines. They gave him cough medicine and Advil in a desperate attempt to bring his fever down. It didn't work. I can't tell you what his exact temperature was but his head was very hot to the touch.

We agreed to use some of the water from rations to keep a cloth wet on his head, but all of our efforts were in vain.

Two days later little Johnny was dead.

It was a hard time for all of us. Mostly them but I did actually like the kid. Judy stayed in her room and cried a lot while Ron sat at the table wallowing in his own self pity.

Together with Ron I grabbed the sheet-wrapped little body and laid it inside one of the holes in the small room. We had kind of a half-assed funeral, well really just a bawl-fest and then Ron and I took turns to cover him up.

I was laying in bed reading later that night when my door slowly opened. Judy walked in as I sat up. She walked over to me, knelt down in front of where I was sitting, looked me in the eyes and whispered. "I need this." Tears filled her eyes as she took off her clothes. She reached down and pulled off my shorts. As reluctant as I was, I was not going to deny her what she wanted.

She pushed me down onto my back, climbed up on the bed and straddled me. She rode me slowly, softly sighing her pleasure. I felt the gentle rain of her tears on my chest as she satisfied some kind of need I could never understand. I could feel her contractions as repeated orgasms rocked her body. At one point while my eyes were open I saw Ron standing in the doorway watching us. I thought for sure he would come in and stop us but instead he just walked away, a look of absolute defeat on his face.

She laid down on top of me when we were finished and whispered to me that she loved me. I can't remember if I said anything back or not but I do know that we both fell asleep. It was the first time I slept next to a woman since Anna had left and God forgive me, I liked it.

When I woke in the morning she was gone from my side. I laid there for a moment unsure of what to expect when I left the room. When I finally got up, I opened the door to my room only to reveal that Judy was sitting at the table alone. When she looked at me her eyes seemed empty. She looked from me to the door to her room then back again. Without her saying a word I knew before I looked inside what I was going to find when I did.

I walked over and opened the door to her room that she shared with her husband, only to find him dangling from one of the wooden beams in the ceiling. He had used his belt, his neck had purple bruising around it and his head lolled off to one side. His eyes were still open, and they seemed to be looking at me, accusing me.

"I guess he couldn't take the thought of going on without Johnny." Judy said from the table.

I was about to say something when I realized that she hadn't seen him in the doorway. She thought losing his son was what drove him to do this. I figured it was the thought of losing everything he had left that had made him do what he did. Not only did he watch his son die, but he also thought he lost his wife to another man.

I carefully took him down and wrapped him in the sheet from their bed. When I came out of the room she was still sitting at the table. I can still remember the vacant expression on her face.

Together we managed to drag his body to the other room and slide it into one of the two remaining holes. She helped me bury him, and by the time we were done we were both exhausted. I went and laid in my bed and a minute later she joined me, and we slept.

I don't know how long she slept for. When I got up she was standing and staring into what was once their room. When I figured things out, it turned out I had slept for about twenty two hours. I was famished. I went to the food closet and got us double rations. I figured not only did we deserve it right now but also as bad as it sounds there were two less mouths to feed. I needed to get my mind off of everything that had happened the last two days so I spent a couple hours after that figuring out the rations for the time we had left.

The next year went by very quickly. Now that it was down to just the two of us, there was no need to be discreet. We spent most of our time in the nude. We were like a reborn Adam and Eve only this was no garden of eden.

When it came to the point where we were down to two weeks worth of food, we had been in the shelter for four years, three months and twenty three days. I finally decided It was time to get out of there.

When we were ready, I pulled the key from under my mattress, walked over and unlocked the door. I waited a moment, took a deep breath and tried the door. At first the door wouldn't open, but it finally relented and swung open on its hinges with a loud squeal.

The heat was intense but bearable as it washed over my body the way a six foot wave would wash over you if you were standing waist deep in the Atlantic Ocean. It was hard to breathe for the first couple of seconds, but my lungs quickly got used to it. Outside the door my house was gone. Other than a small amount of junk and garbage in what was left of my basement there was no indication that a house ever stood here.

It was dark out here as well. Not full dark like night, but almost. There seemed to be kind of a film around the planet filled with dust particles. This is another thing that was predicted by some scientists. There was enough dust in the outer atmosphere that it was blocking the suns rays from fully reaching the earth. Yet there was no dust in the air that was filling my lungs. The ground was another story. Dust or dirt, whichever it was, was about two inches thick on everything.

I noticed that the stairs leading up to what used to be the back yard were still intact, so I walked over to them and began to climb. When I was halfway up I could see over the basement wall so I stopped and had a look around. I turned in a complete circle and could not see a building at all in any direction. With the day being so dim I really couldn't see too far but I assumed that there was nothing standing for miles. There was debris everywhere, from what was left of houses to pieces of vehicles.

I looked back to see where Judy was, but I didn't see her anywhere. I climbed back down the stairs and looked in the shelter door. She was sitting at the table wringing her hands together. I asked her why she wasn't coming out and she told me she was too scared. I went in and sat next to her at the table. I told her that there didn't seem to be anything to be afraid of. She had agreed to that but then said that she just wasn't ready to venture out yet. I told her I understood but that I wanted to go out and look around a little. She asked if I was sure, which I was. She reluctantly agreed that maybe it was a good idea but she wanted to wait until tomorrow. I disagreed, so we came to an understanding that I would go alone but not far, or for very long.

I turned away and again climbed the stairs. This time I made it to the top and walked into what was once my back yard. I walked toward the street and was surprised to find some houses were actually still standing.

The shape they were in remained to be seen. Everywhere I walked I was kicking up dust so I started to look for footprints or any other indication in the dust that another person, or animal for that matter might be alive. In the two blocks I walked, I saw and heard nothing.

Sometimes in life we take certain things for granted and we ignore them. We never give them a second thought until they are not there. Birds chirping, crickets singing, even the sound of traffic going by. Those are all things you can tone out on a daily basis, but today I would have given anything to hear even just one of those sounds.

I had walked two blocks to the corner of Imperial and Rose Streets. I stood in the middle of the intersection and looked at what I had come down here for. This was where the grocery store was and to my delight it was still here. I decided to go back and get Judy before venturing in.

When I returned she was still sitting at the table but had stopped the nervous wringing of her hands. She was just waiting and staring at the door expectantly. When I entered she let out a sigh of what I assumed was relief and she later told me it was.

I told her about what I had found with the houses and the store. I asked her if she wanted to go and check out some of the houses to see if maybe there was another place to stay that was actually above ground. She told me she would rather stay in the shelter another night because she wasn't ready to leave yet. She was scared.

I asked her what she was afraid of and told her that I had not seen any sign of any living thing out there. She told me that that was exactly what she was afraid of. She was afraid of going out into the world and finding nothing. Finding that she might be the last woman on earth was more than she thought she could handle.

I told her I understood and that we could stay in the shelter for one more night. Later, after she went to bed, I took one of the chairs from the table and took it out into the basement and sat down. I stared up into the starless sky for a long time that first night. I don't know what I was hoping for. Maybe for the dust to clear so I could see the stars, maybe for an airplane to fly overhead, or maybe just for a bird to come by and shit on my face. Whatever it was I waited for, I went back inside disappointed.

In the morning I convinced her to come out with me. We stood together in the middle of what had been our street. For some reason it seemed lighter than it did the day before but it must have been just a trick of the mind because absolutely nothing had changed. The only signs of life were my tracks from the day before. We walked down the street together looking for a house that might still be in good enough shape for us to stay in.

We had made it about half a block when she suddenly stopped. She was looking at a small house that was set back from the road. The place looked almost fully intact except for the windows which had all been blown out. We left the road and walked over to the front door. I told her to wait outside while I went in to look around and make sure that it was safe. She insisted on coming with me so we went inside together.

We moved slowly but systematically through the house and found it to be structurally sound. There was furniture as well. Of course it was all covered in dust, but it was nothing that a little cleaning wouldn't take care of. We agreed that this would be a place to stay for a while until we decided on what our next move was going to be. We agreed that she would stay and clean up a little while I went back to the shelter and grabbed a couple days worth of supplies.

When I returned a couple hours later she had gotten most of the floors swept with a broom she had found in a closet, she had flipped the mattress, and was in the process of cleaning the living room furniture. I brought the supplies in, set them on the table in the kitchen, and then got to helping her clean. When we were done for the day, the house had actually started to look fairly decent in the dim light. We had gotten everything somewhat clean and had put our supplies away in the cupboards. We went to the bedroom and made the bed with blankets I had brought from the shelter.

As I got undressed and climbed into bed she turned and closed the bedroom door before getting undressed herself.

It started with the giggles but very quickly full blown laughter overtook me. She looked at me confused until she had realized what it was she had done and then she suddenly burst into laughter along with me. When we finally settled ourselves down and she climbed into bed, we made love.

This experience was different than any other time we had been together. There was a passion to our lovemaking that had never been there before. Maybe it was the fact that after four years, we were out and alive. Or maybe it was just getting some normalcy back. Whatever it was we both climaxed harder than ever before and then just slumped together and fell asleep, exhausted.

We stayed in that house for over a year. It was clean, it was nice and it was a home. Even though there was just the two of us, we were making the best of things. The days were getting a little lighter and you could now see the silhouette of the sun in the sky. Every morning I would try the radio stations. Everyday one of us would venture to the grocery store to find some food that was still good, and every night we would sit out together and stare at the sky.

One day I was reading when it was her turn to go to the store. I must have nodded off and when I woke, the light from the day was fading and she still had not returned. She was never gone for this long. My curiosity getting the best of me I headed down to the store to find her and see if she needed a hand.

A feeling of dread came over me as I entered the store because there was a silence hanging in the air that can't be described with words. I rushed through the store calling out her name until I found her. She must have been climbing the shelves to reach something at the top, because she was now laying in the middle of the aisle, eyes wide open, in a pool of coagulating blood.

I dropped to my knees and cried. I cried for hours. I cried for little Johnny, I cried for Ron, I cried for Judy, I cried for the rest of the earth's population. Mostly I cried for myself.

I was alone.

As far as I knew I was the last person alive on the planet and I didn't know what to do.

After my pity party was over, I trudged home and collapsed into bed.

The next morning I got out of bed, went through my radio routine and then ate until I was stuffed. I then grabbed a backpack from the front door. I loaded up some supplies, changed into a pair of hiking boots I had found in one of the other houses and made my way out. I had decided sometime over breakfast that it was time to get busy living or get busy dying. I decided I would rather live and started walking.

I've been walking ever since that day. For two years just walking, eating, sleeping and wishing. I still sit every night and stare at the sky. I decided long ago that it's not stars I'm looking for anymore. Seeing the stars would only mean that the sky is getting clearer. What I really want to see is an airplane. An airplane is a sign of life. A sign that I am not alone. A sign that somewhere, civilization has continued.

I have decided that there is no possible way that I am the last one alive. There were so many people smarter than me. There had to be someone somewhere. If there was anyone out there, I was going to find them.

A few nights ago I saw one. I was drifting in and out of sleep but I know I saw one. There's no way I had dreamed it.

As I sit here now writing this letter, I am sitting outside looking into the night sky again.

Hoping to see one again.

Wishing to see one again.

Praying to see an airplane.

# Goodbye, My Love

*By Tom*

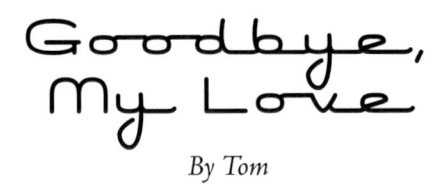

She asks me to stay.

She begs me to remain by her side.

She pleads for a miracle.

But no one answers.

No one will heed to her calls.

The lines of fate have been drawn and plucked, uncoiling around our feet.

It tears and claws at my core, watching this woman, my love, battle with this reality.

I have experienced love, its roots strong and deep, spreading and growing with passion and warmth.

But my heart has been tricked.

Fire has been unleashed upon it, burning with an unconquerable flame, spreading across everything that once was and could have been.

It cries out in despair, praying with every last beat that these two linked souls not be split apart.

Stay strong, my love.

The machine next to the bed beeps suddenly. We look up as the number on the heart monitor goes down.

Our eyes lock, and I fight back the frustration and tears as I bear witness to the fear inside of her.

Consuming her.

I curse the Gods in silence.

What reason could there be?

Whose need does it serve?

There is no reply, just a heavy calm interrupted by the occasional blips and drips of the machinery around us.

We are completely alone in our sadness; abandoned and left to fend for ourselves.

It had begun like any lover's once upon a time.

There were two main characters, each hopeful for something new, each unaware of their real destiny.

There were doubts, obstacles and other paths that each could have taken, but true love proved strong and prevailed.

But there was no happily ever after.

Fate had thrown a final twist, one from which we could not recover.

The tiniest of giants had settled in, harbouring beneath the skin, unnoticed, slowly destroying the body from within.

It had been a slow process, the sickness crawling leisurely throughout its victim.

But now it had complete control, and it quickened its pace.

Its victory was near.

Stay strong, my love.

She looked to me again, holding out her hand for mine.

I took it gently, placing each finger between hers.

I smiled, but she did not return it.

I watched her body tremble, felt her grip tighten on my hand, the skin on her knuckles going white.

And that's when I saw the tear slipping down the side of her pale cheeks, coming to a stop at the edge of her chin.

I felt my heart break instantly, crushed by the sight of this angel in such agony.

Be strong, my love.

I took my free hand, placing her face in my palm, begging her for a smile.

There were things left unfinished. Goals and desires left unattained.

A home. A pet. A child.

The doctor walked in, nodding to both of us as he checked each machine, scribbling notes on a clipboard.

He made his way over to us.

Stopping next to her, he leaned in and whispered into her ear.

She began to cry again, burying her face in her hands.

I know what he said to her.

Taking her hand once more, I raised it to my face, kissing each finger.

It's alright, my love.

It's OK.

She rose to her feet, the tears flowing freely, bent down, and placed a kiss on my forehead.

I smiled back, as she walked with the doctor over to the door.

At the doorway, she stops and turns around to face me.

We stare at one another, silently; two lovers unable to say what they know had to be said.

With a final glance, she exits the room, her sobs echoing through the halls.

I sit here, alone, when the pain suddenly begins to ripple through my body.

I clench my teeth, counting the seconds until the hurt subsides.

Powerless to stop it, I feel myself shaking uncontrollably, the grief overtaking every sense that remains.

As darkness closes in, I struggle to keep my mind clear, fighting to focus on her.

Her beauty.

Her devotion.

Just her.

I close my eyes, ready for Death to take my hand.

Goodbye, my love.

# Looking Back
### By Tom

Looking back, he knew something was wrong.

Less than thirty minutes ago, Leonard Sharp had been sitting in his cubicle at work, his eyes peeking at the clock on the wall every five minutes.

*Get me the hell outa here*, he thought miserably.

Grabbing the coffee mug on his desk, he lifted it to his lips, taking a sip of the now cold coffee inside it.

Putting it back down, he glanced at the writing on its side and scowled.

**Benson and Davis Co.**

**Where dreams can happen.**

Leonard took a deep breath, counting down the seconds until midnight.

He had been working for Benson and Davis Co. for the last six years.

And had been miserable for…oh…say…all six of them.

*It wasn't supposed to have happened like this*, he thought.

He had completed his education.

Worked his ass off his entire life.

Graduated near the top of his class.

Had nailed his interview.

And now, because of all that hard work, his prayers had been answered.

Or so he had thought.

Within days of his new employment, Leonard had found out the hard way what it meant to be the new guy.

Taking notes down.

Mostly for coffee or bagels.

Running across the street to the bakery.

Placing an order for those coffees and bagels.

Sitting in on conferences and meetings.

Listening to the complaints about the coffees and bagels.

Fast forward six years.

No longer a new guy.

Still running the same damn errands.

But he had graduated up a class.

Now it was coffees and sandwiches.

Sometimes they even asked for croissants.

Just to keep him on his toes.

And yet Leonard had never stood up and shouted "No more!"

He had never asked for something more to do.

His family and friends called him a coward.

He thought of it more as a comfort zone.

He had dug himself into a groove.

Placed himself into a regular routine.

It may not be the most comfortable, but it still paid the bills.

With ten minutes left to go, Leonard made a decision that had never once entered his mind before: He grabbed his jacket and briefcase, shot the middle finger to the clock and left work before he was even finished his report for the next morning.

It wouldn't be long until he would be begging for those ten minutes back.

Leonard flicked a dial and watched as the front and rear wipers increased in speed, moving in sync with one another as they fought off the onslaught of rain.

*It figures*, he thought.

Not a damn cloud in the sky all day.

Soon as I get off, it's pissin' rain.

Leonard slowed the car down at the intersection as the stoplights turned yellow.

With the car stopped, Leonard turned the radio off and massaged his temples.

*What a day*, he thought.

After a few moments the lights turned green and Leonard stepped on the gas.

Hell, he thought. *What a life.*

He was sick of it.

Sick of everything.

His job.

His house.

His crappy car.

Most of all, he was sick of being called a coward.

Especially by his own flesh and blood.

He suddenly caught a flash of something in his rear-view mirror and looked up.

Looking back, he noticed a car was coming up swiftly behind him.

Leonard scowled.

*It's late, the roads are practically empty and this jackass feels the need to speed.*

Embracing the urge to be a prick, he stared at his speedometer, levelling his speed off to the legal limit.

*Either pass me or slow down, asshole*, he thought, smiling to himself.

To Leonard's surprise, the car did indeed slow down, and more than ten feet away from his own car.

"Smart ass," he said aloud.

Seeing the red light ahead, he began to slow down his car, making sure to watch the guy behind him.

Sitting at the lights, Leonard looked around.

There was hardly a soul out and about tonight, save for a few drivers here and there.

He looked into his mirror again, just as an array of lightning bolts lit up the sky.

The car was sitting a good five to ten feet back from him, but it was in that flash of lightning that allowed Leonard the briefest glimpse inside their car.

There were two people in the car, Leonard noticed.

A man and a woman.

And it looked like they were arguing.

The man was in the passenger's seat and appeared to be shouting.

The woman, behind the wheel, looked almost bored, avoided eye contact, completely inattentive to what the man was saying.

*Married life*, Leonard thought to himself. *What a headache.*

He had no time for love, and had almost thirty years of single life to prove it.

The light turned green and he continued forward.

The car followed, sticking close to Leonard's car.

*But not too close*, he thought curiously, unsure why the vehicle behind him was rousing his interest.

He also began to notice how the car was suddenly slowing, as though the driver had caught on to Leonard's curiosity.

Suddenly, as though trying to avoid an array of animals on the road, the car began to swerve madly, left into the opposite lane, and then right, grinding against the curb.

*What the hell*, Leonard thought.

But just as quickly as it happened, the car went back on path, once again calmly driving in a straight line, a mere three to five feet behind him.

What the hell was that about? He wondered.

Looking ahead, Leonard almost missed the stop sign, resulting in an extended series of screeches and skids as both cars jammed on their brakes.

His heart racing, Leonard rolled down his window and was just about to throw his hand out the window for an apologetic wave, when something caught his eye in the rear-view mirror again.

Because the car had stopped so close behind Leonard's car, his brake lights were shining directly at the car's windshield behind him.

Behind the glass, Leonard watched as the couple behind him were locked in some sort of struggle.

Their arms were joined together in some sort of twisted pretzel, both of them fixated on an object each tried to pry out of the other's hands.

The man's teeth were bared, expressing focus and fury, while the woman looked as though she was crying, a look of complete terror on her face.

Leonard squinted hard, bringing his eyes closer to his mirror.

A gun.

*Oh, God*, he thought.

Feeling his stomach drop our from under him, Leonard's gaze shifted, staring straight out at the road ahead.

*What do I do?* He thought, his mind racing.

Before he could even think of an answer, his foot took over, stepping down on the gas.

*There's nothing you can do*, his mind reasoned with him. *Just get the hell out of here.*

Leonard looked down at the speedometer, as his speed went twenty over the limit.

Out of view from the other car, Leonard pulled over to the side of the road and rolled down the window.

Gulping in fresh air, he tried calming his nerves.

"He's going to kill her," he said aloud.

*It's none of your business.*

"But I could have done something."

*Oh? Like what?*

"Something."

*You mean like getting yourself killed too?*

"I could have tried something. Anything."

*The man has a gun.*

"But she's going to die."

*Yes. But the coward will live another day.*

Breaking out of his trance, Leonard screamed out in anger.

"No!"

*No?*

"I'm not a coward!"

Leonard threw the car in drive, stamped down on the gas and sped back toward the other car.

I'm so sick of the way they all talk about me.

Ask for a raise Leonard.

Tell your boss off Leonard.

Don't be a coward Leonard.

He looked into his rear-view mirror, catching himself smile.

Who's the coward now?

What will they all say about meek, obedient Leonard now?

As he caught sight of the other car's headlights in the distance, he felt a tightening in his chest as his breathing became heavier.

What's the plan Leonard?

Going to scream at the guy and hope he drops the gun and runs?

Unless she's already dead and he's long gone.

He stepped harder on the gas pedal, increasing the car's speed.

No.

Don't think like that.

Looking ahead, Leonard gasped.

The man was getting out of the car.

As Leonard continued to watch, the man walked around the side of the car, stopping at the driver's side door.

Completely oblivious to Leonard approaching, the man raised his right arm, the gun clutched tightly in his hand.

He pointed it at the woman inside.

Without a thought, without a plan, Leonard switched into the opposite lane, turned on his high beams and slammed his foot down, gathering as much speed as the car would allow him.

The man looked over, attempting to swing his arm around to face the oncoming car.

But it was too late.

Leonard closed his eyes as the two cars grinded together, sending sparks into the air.

He heard a sickening thump as the car connected with the man's body.

A smash as something hit the windshield.

The sound of something rolling on the top of his car.

Leonard jammed on his brakes, skidding a few feet before coming to a stop.

His heart pounded with the intent to break free from his chest.

Looking back, he saw the driver's side door open, a woman's legs coming out of it.

Although still in shock, Leonard put the car in park, took off his seatbelt and forced himself out of the car and on to the rain-slicked road.

"Ma'am!" He shouted. "Ma'am, are you ok?"

The woman got out, a look of disbelief and confusion evident on her face.

"You?" she finally stammered. "You did this?"

With both cars still running and the street lamps on each side of the street shining brightly, Leonard was able to take in the woman's appearance.

She was astonishingly beautiful.

She was tall, with curves a goddess would die for.

She wore a tight black skirt down to her knees, topped with a white, short-sleeved dress shirt.

Her dark hair flowed in waves, decorating her glowing, porcelain-like skin.

He couldn't make out her eyes, but even the look of alarm on her face could silence a room.

"Everything's alright now," he said, stopping a few feet from her. "Do you have a cell phone? I don't have one, but we need to call the cops."

She shook her head, and as her hair moved to the side, Leonard saw the gash on her forehead.

"Ma'am, you're hurt," he said, concerned. "Did he hit you?"

She nodded.

"I'm fine though," she said softly. "But I think he had a phone in his pocket."

Leonard looked over at the man's crumpled body, less than ten feet from them.

"Right," he said. "You sit tight and I'll get some help here."

He slowly made his way over to the still figure on the ground, worried as though at any moment he would spring to his feet, pointing a gun at Leonard's chest.

"What's your name?" she asked from behind him.

"Leonard Sharp."

"Why did you do come back, Leonard?"

He knelt beside the man, too afraid to feel for a pulse.

"It's a long story," he replied, nervously checking the man's pockets.

"Please?" she asked.

A few seconds passed before Leonard could answer.

"I don't really know," he replied, "I guess I was just sick of being the coward. I just couldn't keep driving."

"I'm very grateful," she said.

Finding nothing in the man's jacket, Leonard padded the man's pants pockets.

Wallet.

Car keys.

No cell phone.

Scanning the area, Leonard came to another realization.

*Where's the gun?* He thought.

"Well, there's no phone," he said, still searching the ground around him. "But I think there's a gas station a couple miles up from here, we can call from there."

Opening up the man's wallet, he came across some pictures.

Two young boys and a baby girl.

A woman draped around a man.

A woman and a man surrounded by the three children.

Leonard put the wallet back down, the pictures playing over and over in his head.

This guy had a family.

What the hell was he doing with this chick?

CLICK.

The horrifying sound of a gun being cocked filled the air.

A vision came back to him.

Less than twenty minutes ago.

A struggle.

A man and woman in a car, locked in a struggle for a gun.

No.

A man struggling to grab it from the woman.

The look of terror and desperation on his face.

The deranged, confident look on hers.

"You know, it's amazing what a man will do for a helpless woman," she said suddenly, snapping him back to reality.

Leonard's stomach somersaulted.

*Oh God, no*, he thought. *Please, no.*

Turning to face her, he found himself staring into the barrel of a gun.

The woman holding it no longer looked beautiful. She had a crazed look to her, an insane smile that went dangerously close to her eyes.

"I'd like you to know, Leonard, that I don't think you're a coward."

Frozen on his knees, he could only watch as she put her finger on the trigger.

"Let's just call you unlucky."

# 24 Hour Marathon

*By Chris*

It was the greatest thing I had ever seen. From the first time I saw it, right up until I was on it, I was obsessed.

24 Hour Marathon.

It's the highest rated game show/reality show on t.v. with over four billion viewers worldwide every month. The show airs on the first Monday of every month, with repeats showing every following Monday. Even the reruns get an amazing amount of viewers. Best of all, the winner gets twenty five million dollars.

The idea of the show is simple. Twenty five contestants compete in twenty four events over a twenty four hour period. One person is eliminated following each event, leaving one winner at the end.

The best part of the entire show though, is the eliminations themselves. They make every elimination look like a death. The special effects make it look so realistic that you would think that you were watching the real thing.

Sometimes for the new episodes we would have twenty four hour parties with multiple t.v.s tuned in around the house. Those were always fun and feisty because not only were we all watching the show but we were all betting on who was going to be eliminated during each event as well.

I had been wanting to go on the show ever since the first time I saw it. I'm not the only one though, everyone I know had applied to be on the show, and when I actually got the call, I received a lot of support from everyone, after they were done being jealous of course.

As word of my acceptance onto the show had spread, I was asked a lot of questions by my friends and family about what I was going to be doing, what my elimination was going to be like, but I just didn't have the answers. No two shows ever had the same events. In fact, in all the episodes I had watched, I had never seen the same event twice.

You just didn't know beforehand what the events were going to be.

They had thousands of different events, all printed on a small piece of paper, which is placed inside a small plastic ball, which is then placed inside a large drum. The drum is mixed up and events are chosen by pulling balls out at random and reading the paper inside.

There was no way to actually prepare for the show. It was good to be in great physical shape, because some of the events involved strength, some endurance, but some involved just plain luck. I guess it didn't really matter though because if they wanted you to win, you won.

* * *

They had flown me in on a commercial airline but had at least put me in first class. I felt like royalty on that flight. I was given food, drinks, pillows, anything I asked for. I don't know if I will ever fly anything but first class again.

I arrived at The Bowl at around nine a.m. on the day of the show, with the show starting at midnight. The Bowl is the place where the events are held and the show is filmed. It had been built to be an exact replica of one of the old Roman Coliseums, and as far as I could tell, it was. It was absolutely spectacular.

As soon as I arrived I was ushered into an office where I had to fill out mountains of paperwork. There were liability forms, insurance forms, next of kin forms, mostly I guess if there was some sort of accident that caused injury or death. Others came into the room too, and began filling out the same mountainous piles of forms. Assuming they were my competition I started sizing them up.

Men, women, all races, all sizes, some looked tough, others looked fast. Among these people I felt I was about average, my size and strength was nothing to brag about, but I felt good.

After the paperwork, I was shown around The Bowl. Of particular interest to me was the event area and the holding room. Events were just like in the day of gladiators, played in a giant circle of sand. The holding room was nothing but a square room, with one continuous bench lining three of the four walls. In one corner was a crude toilet for all of us to use when we needed to.

After the tour I was ushered to a comfortable room, where I was to stay until game time. I was asked what I wanted for dinner, and when I replied spaghetti and meatballs, they laughed at me. We were allowed to have anything we wanted. Anything at all, but spaghetti was my favorite, so that was what I wanted.

At eleven, they came for me.

At eleven thirty I was ushered into the holding room with all the other contestants.

Nobody talked. I tried to lighten the mood and talk to a couple of others but for the most part everyone just ignored me. I wondered who was going to be eliminated first, and how it was going to be done. Would it look less realistic in person? When was my elimination? Nobody had talked to me about it yet. I just hoped that when it happened it would look really cool and I hoped I would be convincing enough. I couldn't wait to be back home watching reruns with my friends and watching myself die. I guess it would be like an actor watching his own movie.

At eleven fifty five we were led out into the event area. The crowd roared. Fifty thousand people were here to see this take place live. The noise was almost deafaning. At twelve midnight the show went live on the air.

After a brief introduction by the show's host outlining the rules for the contest, the first event was drawn.

There was only one word on the paper when it was taken from the ball.

Race.

I heard a murmur among us contestants, as the ones who were good runners expressed their delight, while the ones who were not expressed their displeasure.

We were led to the edge of the sand and given our instructions.

We were to run around the perimeter of the event area. At the end of the hour, whoever was the slowest would be eliminated. If anyone was lapped, they would be eliminated and the event would be over as soon as that happened.

I wasn't too concerned about this one. Although I wasn't giving any instructions about what I was supposed to do concerning my elimiation, I just assumed it wasn't supposed to be here.

I could hear one of the other contestants muttering under his breath that he was going to go all out and try to lap someone as fast as he could so he could rest before the next event.

After our instruction, we were lined up, then given the signal to run. Right away the muttering guy broke out and ran as fast as he could. A couple others tried to follow suit, but he was really quick.

I had decided to stay around mid pack. Since it was only the first lapped person or the slowest after an hour who was eliminated I figured it was as safe a place as any to be. I kept looking over my shoulder to see if I was losing any ground, but I wasn't, and then suddenly that was when it hit me.

Cramp.

I almost fell over with the severity of it. We were about twenty minutes in when it happened. The leader was gaining on the last place guy quickly now, so I decided to try to walk it off for a second. Most of the contestants were slow now, a couple of the others were walking as well.

Then suddenly the crowd started to roar.

The leader had almost caught one of the walkers. Hearing the crowd he turned to look and when he saw the leader bearing down on him he took off. Within a split second, everyone near the back was suddenly coming at me fast. So was the leader.

So I ran.

I wasn't as fast as I was before, but I ran.

The crowd was getting louder now.

I was passed by two runners.

I looked over my shoulder to see I was losing ground.

The crowd got louder, anticipating the onset of an elimination, they were whipping themselves into a frenzy.

I was passed by two more.

I looked back again and saw there was only one other guy behind me, with the leader running him down. I tried to go faster, I really did, but my body was done.

I was passed again. It was the leader.

A shot rang out.

It was loud even within the noise of the crowd.

All the runners stopped.

I turned and looked. Only a few steps behind me was a man laying face down in the dirt. There was a bullet hole in the back of his head, and blood pooling around the front. Looking at him laying there, I couldn't tell how they had made it look so real.

He must have been only a step or two behind me when he was passed by the leader.

"ELIMINATED." The crowd roared.

One down, twenty three more to go.

We were taken into the holding room where we all collapsed on the benches. It was twelve thirty so we had a half hour to rest. We heard the announcement of the next event over the p.a. system.

Weights.

We came back out at twelve fifty five. We were led to the center of the event area where they had some contraptions set up.

There were twenty four leg press machines set up. We were each led to one, then the machines were adjusted to fit each one of its occupants. The presses were each holding up a five hundred pound weight. The top of the weight had a chain fastened to it which went up over a pulley then back down to a collar which was placed around each contestants neck. The premise being that the first person unable to hold the weight up would appear to be hung when their legs gave out. There was a kill switch that disconnected all the remaining chains when the elimination was decided.

When everyone was in their seats and everything was adjusted, they took the safeties off the weights.

My legs held solid under the sudden pressure of the weight. I felt good. I felt like I could hold it for the entire hour, or longer. I relaxed in my seat as much as I could. It actually didn't feel like five hundred pounds at all. I wondered if some of the smaller men and women had even lighter weights than I had.

I looked around a bit at the others. The machines were set up in a circle, so we could all see each other. One of the smaller girls was struggling. We were only five minutes in, and already I could see that her legs were shaking, and beads of sweat were standing out on her forehead.

Her eyes locked on mine. She was a great actress too, because it really did appear that she was terrified of dropping the weight.

Then suddenly, she was jerked hard out of her seat. She was now hanging from the machine, legs kicking and arms flailing. I heard the chains fall from the other machines, including my own. I released the weight and stood up.

I watched as the hanging girl's movements slowed and then finally stopped. I hadn't noticed but the crowd had become almost silent. Her body finally went limp and the crowd erupted.

"ELIMINATED!"

I took a look around, and I don't think I saw a single person actually sitting in their seat. They were thriving on this, caught up in the excitement. They were insatiable. I think if they had their way they would sit through this for weeks on end and not just twenty four hours.

It was only one fifteen, and we were being led back to the holding room. Lots of time to rest. I was feeling really great about myself and I think some of the others were as well.

* * *

I was still in when we were brought back out at six o'clock for an event called Bubble Bath. I had been around through six eliminations but so had eighteen others.

There was a large tank now set up in the middle of the bowl with a platform overtop of it. We were led up a set of stairs onto the platform.

We were instructed on how the event would work. To break it down, it was basically just a long jump competition. In turn we all ran and jumped as far as we could. After that first round of jumping, I was in the top half of the contestants. When everyone had finally finished their first jump, they began to alter the platform.

The shortest jump was only five feet, five inches, so there was now a gap in the platform measuring that exact distance. The opening, if you were to come up short, was going to drop you into the tank below. Inside the tank, the water had been made to looke like it was being kept at a steady boil.

In trying to figure this one out, the only thing I could think of was that they had some underwater fans forcing the water to bubble on top.

The woman who's jump was the shortest began to cry and panic, and she was made to go first. She was a good actress too. At first she refused but after appearing to be tended to with cattle prods she took her turn. She ran and jumped with everything she had and cleared the distance easily.

The water down below was splashing up onto the jumping surface. Two jumpers before it was my turn to go, one of the men pretended to slip in the water, and ended up jumping short. His head looked like it hit the edge of the platform on the other side and he fell down into the water.

"ELIMINATED!" Once again the crowd shouted.

I looked into the tank and saw the man floating in the moving water. I was actually surprised by how long he was able to hold his breath.

We were led back down into the holding room as the next event was drawn.

* * *

When noon rolled around fatigue was starting to set in for some of us. We were hungry, thirsty and sore. Even though they were staged, the events were really starting to take their toll. We were now entering the arena for an event called arrows.

As I walked out I scanned the crowd. I could see that some of the children had drifted off to sleep in their seats, while their parents were still enjoying the show. Even after twelve hours I could still not find an empty seat anywhere that I looked.

The remaining thirteen of us were told to stand in a circle. The circle was around one hundred feet across. We stood there as a man carrying a bow walked into the center of us all. He had on his back a quiver of arrows.

I had to surpress a laugh as Robin Hood came to mind.

The archer then reached into his pocket, pulled out a blindfold, and put it on. He stood waiting as men came up behind us and put blindfolds on us as well. We were then told that the archer would spin himself and stop at random intervals to fire the bow. He would continue to do this until one of us was eliminated.

There were tense moments as the crowd had once again fallen dead silent. I could hear the shuffle of the archer's feet as he spun himself, the stretching of the bow as he pulled back, and the TWANG as he released it.

There were a couple of shots that were close enough for me to hear the arrow whiz past me. I remember smiling everytime I heard one go by. The sound effects guys were good.

I remember the pain when the arrow struck me in the shoulder. It was intense. I had almost been knocked off my feet by the impact. I reached up to feel where the arrow had hit me, wondering why I hadn't been told beforehand that I was going to be hit. If they would have told me, then I would have been prepared to play it up more.

When my hand reached where the arrow was I could feel a warm sticky mess.

And that was when the realization suddenly came to me.

THIS WAS REAL!

There were no sound guys, no special effects, people were really being killed.

The crowd had cheered when I had been hit but now settled back down and I could hear the shuffling feet again. After a few moments, a cheer thundered out again.

"ELIMINATED!"

I took off my blindfold to see that one of the guys on the other side of the circle was down on the ground with an arrow sticking out of his throat.

He's really dead.

Thirteen people eliminated.

Eleven more to come.

These were the thoughts racing through my head as we were led back to the holding room.

Medics came in and patched me up as best they could within the small amount of time they had. I was in shock as well as being shot by the arrow.

Never in all the time watching the show had I ever considered that the deaths might be real.

\* \* \*

Six o'clock.

Eighteen eliminations done, six more to go. I was still hanging in, but barely. The last couple eliminations had been really close, but I had lucked our for a couple events.

The seven of us were led out for an event called Gaunlet.

We were led to one end of the arena and told to form a line. I ended up third in line. At the time I was just happy that I wasn't first.

A gate at the other end opens up and scores of people are led into the arena. They form two lines down the middle of the event area. I was so fascinated with the people that I didn't notice each one of them was carrying some sort of weapon. When I did notice it looked to me like they were wooden clubs.

Our instructions were simple. Run down the middle of the two lines of people and make it to the other side. Their instructions were even more simple. When we run, beat us with the clubs.

I was worried now. One hit to my injured shoulder and I would end up going down real quick. I had to hope that one of the first two didn't make it.

My hopes were realized with the first contestant. She went running in but after only about ten feet or so one of the clubs caught her right in the nose. She had gone down on one knee for what was only a split second, but even that was too long. In the time it took her knee to hit the ground, she had been clubbed about the head no less than six more times.

She slumped to the ground and the people in attendace screamed.

"ELIMINATED!"

After a few seconds her head had shattered like a watermelon. We were already being led back by that point, but I remember looking back and seeing the frenzy as they continued to beat her already lifeless body.

Now that it had sunk in that all of this was real, I was in survival mode. Even with my injured shoulder I was still making it through. After each event, my confidence had grown a little actually allowing me to think that maybe I really did have a chance.

I was either going to be twenty five million dollars richer at the end of the day, or I was going to be dead.

\* \* \*

Eleven o'clock.

Three of us left.

Stepping stones was the event.

As we were walking out, I noticed that there were now a number of small, dirt mounds scattered around the arena. We were led to the center of the event area, and given our instructions.

Hidden inside one of the many small mounds scattered about was a landmine. We were each to take turns walking up onto a mound. The one who blows up is eliminated.

My name was drawn first so without hesitation I walked to the nearest mound and stood on top. After a few seconds, one of the others was made to take their turn. He decided to climb one a little further away, and did so without elimination. Finally, the last contestant, who was also the last woman still standing, took her turn and stood on a mound. Every minute, one of us was to move to a new mound.

It was at the twenty two minute mark when the other remaining man climbed up on a mound, and with a loud boom, and a cloud of dust and blood, was no longer there.

The crowd cheered and screamed, "ELIMINATED!"

We were led back to the holding room. Just me and her. It was finally down to two.

When the door shut, I sat on the bench along one wall, looked across, and she was sitting along the opposite wall. Our eyes locked. I could see the fear, excitement, and weariness in her eyes. When she looked back at me, I am sure she saw the same. We kept our eyes locked on each other, neither one of us wavering. We stared at each other for the entire time we were there. No words were spoken, neither one of us would even clear our throat, lest it be a sign of weakness.

When the door opened for us to go out for the final event, neither one of us would move. It wasn't until they came in and grabbed us by the arms that we were forced to break our stare.

We were led to the center of the arena to a thunderous ovation. Looking around, I could see that no one was left sitting once again.

As soon as I saw the contraption we were being led to, all the breath left my body. My knees almost buckled as I remembered the last word I had heard before they had taken us to the holding room the last time.

Blades.

Each of us were led to stand beside a large metal column. On one side of the column at neck height was an arm sticking out with a large blade attached. On the other side was an identicle arm with an identicle blade, but this one was at ankle height.

The idea was simple, the column would spin, and the contestant would have to alternately jump and duck the blades as they came around. The longer the event went, the faster the column would spin.

Our eyes locked again as the columns were set up in a way where we were facing each other during the event.

The columns started. I quickly got into the simple rhythm of jumping over one blade and ducking under the other.

Jump.

Duck.

Jump.

Duck.

She had fallen into the rhythm as well. Our eyes were no longer locked, but every now and then we would catch each others gaze as we looked from one blade to the other.

The blades began to speed up.

Jump, duck, jump, duck.

The pace had quickened, but the rhythm was still pretty easy to keep up with. I could feel the muscles in my legs flexing and relaxing as I jumped and ducked. I knew I had more time left before they gave out but I only hoped it was more time than she had.

After a few more minutes the pace of the blades quickened again.

Jumpduckjumpduckjumpduck.

My legs were failing quick, and that was when it happened.

On one of her landings, she stumbled. She ducked the high blade as it came around but was off balance still for the low one. The blade cut through both of her ankles like they were not even there. She fell to her hands and knees as the high blade passed harmlessly overhead. The low blade came around again. Being on all fours, the blade cut though both thighs and forearms with ease.

She fell flat. She rolled to her back as the high blade passed overhead. Our eyes locked once more as the low blade came back around and sliced her entire body in two.

"ELIMINATED!" Cheered the crowd.

My column stopped, and I was led away and taken up on top of a platform that had been set up nearby.

As cameras flashed and video rolled I was handed one of those giant cardboard cheques. The amount on it was twenty five million dollars.

\* \* \*

I don't watch the show anymore. Everyone I know still applies to be on it. I try to explain to them what it is like. To have to watch the others die first hand. Some of them still think it is nothing but special effects and that I am paid to act this way, but it's not, and I'm not.

I hoped for a long time that I never had to see or be a part of something like that again.

Then the letter came.

It was from the creators of the 24 hour marathon. They were putting together an all sar show of past winners and asked if I wanted to take part. The prize for this show was going to be one hundred million dollars.

Every fibre of my being told me to tear up the letter.

Throw it out.

Burn it.

Anything.

I keep on picking it up and reading it again.

Over and over.

One hundred million dollars.

I think I'll call tomorrow and accept.

# Drive

*Life begins with driving.*

*My new motto*, Danny thought excitedly.

The only way to live was behind the wheel.

Open road.

Open window.

Open world.

Seventeen-year-old Danny Cross switched on his right indicator light and came to a stop at the busy intersection as the lights made their steady ascent to red.

"So how are you feeling?" his driving instructor asked from the passenger seat. "Nerves ok? Feeling confident?"

"Yup," Danny replied, without looking at her.

The truth was, his insides were spinning and tumbling and squirming all over one another, but he blamed it solely on excitement, rather than anxiety or dread.

This was the moment he had been waiting for.

The days of sitting in the passenger seat would soon be over.

He had endured hell to get to this day.

The painfully boring nights spent in a windowless classroom, learning about street signs and safety, while the world outside continued to spin.

The countless times spent driving with his mother, enduring the shrieks and yelps of a nervous parent.

Or the 10 days behind the wheel with a driving instructor, a woman who had no clue on how to interact with a fellow human being, sputtering out random comments like, "That's a nice car" and "Oh, that reminds me of a song"….

*No*, Danny told himself, suppressing a shudder. *I'm ready for this.*

Watching the lights turn green and ignoring the butterflies, Danny took his foot off the brake, placed it on the gas, and began his turn.

"Easy on the gas," his instructor reminded him. "They're going to be watching everything, remember?"

"Sorry," Danny replied.

He wasn't sorry.

"I forgot."

He hadn't forgotten.

But it was the only way to handle the constant reminders of "Easy on the gas."

Reminders from his mother.

Father.

Instructor.

Neighbors.

Crossing guard.

A "lead foot", his mother called it.

Resulting from "an over-eagerness to own the roads", his father had added.

Danny didn't care.

For him, driving meant power.

And power brought rewards.

His friends, who unfortunately all had their licenses before him, were already reaping their rewards.

Sound systems.

Freedom.

Girls.

And oh, the girls!

Didn't matter if the car was a complete beater, in high school if a guy pulls up in a car, the girls still formed a queue.

Heck, over a month ago he had seen one of his own friends pull up around lunchtime in his 'new' 1989 Ford Escort: Three dates planned within the hour.

But I've got them all beat, Danny thought happily.

A few months ago, after a long and boring bus ride from work, he arrived home to find his father in the driveway, leaning against his just washed and waxed pride and joy: a black 1973 Chevrolet Corvette 2-Door Coupe.

"So I've been thinking", he had said.

"About what?" Danny asked. "Guilty conscience for making your only son take the bus home from work?"

"Funny guy," his dad replied. "But no."

"Of course not," Danny said sarcastically. "Then what?"

And that's when it happened.

His father, a big smile on his face, took out the keys to the beauty sitting silently beside them, and dangled the keychain in front of his son's face.

"You get your license first try, she's yours," he said.

Danny's jaw dropped.

"You're kidding."

His father quickly placed the keys back in his pants pocket and placed his arm around his son.

"No joke, little man. I've been thinking about it for a while and…"

Danny never heard another word, his mind quickly taking the backseat as his eyes took in every curve of the gorgeous beast that would be soon be his.

And now that day was here.

His day to collect and, "own the roads".

Danny slowed down as he pulled up to the ministry building where he'd be taking his test.

"Here we are!" His instructor exclaimed excitedly, as Danny put the car in park and turned it off.

*Good observation*, Danny thought, stepping outside and making his way to the front door of the building. *I can see why you're such an asset to the academy.*

"I guess I'll see you in a bit then?" he asked her, not really hoping for an answer.

"You bet!" she replied happily. "Good luck!"

*Don't need luck*, Danny thought. *I've got this.*

After letting a lady inside know that he was here, he was told to go and wait out by the car.

Less than five minutes later, Danny watched as an older woman, probably in her sixties, emerged into the sunlight, a clipboard in her left hand, and a complete lack of emotion on her face.

"Good morning!" Danny said. "How are you?"

"This car is yours, young man?" she answered jadedly, ignoring his question. "Or does it belong to the driving academy?"

"The academy, ma'am."

"Please start the car and put your hazard lights on," she said, without the slightest trace of humanity.

*Miserable broad*, Danny thought, sliding into the car. *I can tell this is going to be fun.*

And that's how the test began.

Danny made sure to monitor his speed, frequently check every mirror and indicate at every light, the vision of the corvette steering his focus.

Less than fifteen minutes later, Danny and the miserable soul beside him were sitting back in the ministry parking lot, the noise of the idling car drowned out by the traffic of thoughts colliding off of one another in his head:

*Did I pass?*

*Did I fail?*

*What's she waiting for?*

*What's she writing?*

*Does she enjoy torturing people?*

*Please tell me something!*

TELL ME!

"So I have your results," she said quietly, silencing the bellowing beast within.

"OK...," Danny replied slowly, unsure what else to say.

The woman put the cap on her pen, and re-attached it to the top of her clipboard.

"Well," she said, "You definitely need to work on your acceleration. There were, on more than one occasion, instances where you put your foot down a little too hard on the gas."

"OK...," Danny replied through gritted teeth.

"But overall," she continued, flipping through her papers, and handing Danny a small stack. "You did quite well. I decided to pass you. Congratulations, young man."

YES! The beast roared.

"Thank you so much," Danny exclaimed, trying to remain calm.

"I would like to remind you, however," the woman said, opening the car door. "Do take your time on the roads, Mr. Cross. Better to get there in one piece, than in the back of an ambulance."

"Yes ma'am," he said with false sincerity.

And with that, she exited the car, oblivious to the less than courteous gesture being pointed at her retreating back.

Danny's world was a blur on the ride back home, overwhelmed in jubilation at his latest triumph.

He had handed the keys over to his instructor, too pumped up to drive another minute in her dump of a car.

He had heard her mutter something once or twice, but in all the excitement and his complete lack of concern for what she had to say, it went unnoticed.

"Congratulations again!" she exclaimed, as they pulled into his driveway a few minutes later. "It's been great hav…"

"Whatever," Danny said quickly, slamming the car door shut.

Fumbling for the house keys in his jeans' pocket, Danny went over the conversation he and his father had over cereal that morning.

"So when do I officially get to drive the car, Dad?" Danny asked with a mouthful of Cheerios.

His father took a long sip of coffee, surveying Danny over the top of the mug.

"Tell you what," he said finally. "You pass today, you and I will take a cruise soon as I get off work."

Danny's spoon dropped out of his hand, clanked off the bowl and landed in his lap.

"I thought you said if I passed, I could have it?"

His father smiled at him.

"I did say that, you're right. But if it's going to be my last night with the girl, I thought the two of us could share the moment together, no?"

Behind them his mother rolled her eyes.

"OK," Danny said gloomily.

But things had changed now.

The beast inside him was writhing with desire.

*Take the keys*, it said.

*He'll never know.*

Danny stood facing the key rack, hanging by the garage door.

*It's true*, he thought. *I could take it for a quick spin and he'll never even know it left the garage.*

Within seconds Danny had made up his mind.

Snatching up his father's keys, he made his way into the garage.

* * *

WOOO! The beast inside him howled, as the Corvette roared beneath him.

*So this is what freedom feels like!* Danny thought excitedly. *I've been missing out!*

With his left hand on the steering wheel and his right on the shifter, Danny threw the car into fourth gear and hit the gas.

*This baby's a god among insects*, he thought.

*And it deserves to be treated like one.*

As he coasted through the main roads, he glanced down the side streets, keeping an eye out for cop cars.

*Not like they'd catch me anyways.*

Looking ahead at the approaching intersection, Danny saw the color green lighting the way and he pressed down harder on the gas.

Less than twenty feet away, the lights above flashed yellow, but Danny, feeling invincible, pushed down on the clutch and switched to fifth gear, gathering speed as he rolled through the junction.

Suddenly, a truck in the opposite lane, left indicator light blinking, started making his turn, somehow unaware of Danny's intentions.

Having no alternative, Danny tested the car's muscle, threw his weight on the gas and swerved slightly to the right, narrowly avoiding the edge of the curb and the front end of the oncoming truck.

Unaffected by the furious honking behind him, Danny caught himself smiling.

*What a rush!*

Continuing his dominance of the gravel beneath him, Danny looked ahead at the lights in the distance, making sure to maintain his speed.

*No need to slow down*, he thought. *They'll move out of my way.*

Feeling a buzz coming from his jacket pocket, Danny fished out his cell phone and read the text:

*From John: Dude, did u pass?!?!?!*

Keeping one eye on the road, Danny quickly texted back:

*U know it! Nevr guess what im driving! Lol*

Danny hit the send button, and watched on the little screen as the message began its journey outward.

Smiling, Danny looked up, just in time to see all hell come crashing down.

All he remembered was a blur of something in front of him, succeeded by the most horrifying BAM! that echoed over and over in his head.

Slamming down on the brakes, he felt the car grinding and squealing beneath his feet as it struggled to get a grip on the pavement.

His heart beating louder and louder with every passing second, Danny held his breath until the car finally came to a stop.

Terrified and gasping for air, Danny sat frozen and pale in the driver's seat.

*Oh my god*, he thought. *What the hell was that?*

Looking down, Danny watched as his hands fidgeted with the straps of his seatbelt.

*I have to know.*

Ignoring the sickness welling up inside of him, Danny unclasped his seatbelt, opened the door and made his way out of the car.

Standing up straight, he inhaled deeply, trying to calm his nerves.

Closing the car door, Danny walked slowly towards the front of the car.

*A cat*, he thought. *That's what it was.*

*Maybe a dog.*

Looking down, Danny noticed a small pool of gasoline forming near his feet.

*Wait a minute*, he thought.

*Oh God no.*

As he bent down to get a closer look, a picture began to form itself in Danny's mind.

Blood.

It was blood.

*Oh God no.*

*Please no.*

Danny rose to his feet, and started to back away towards his car door.

But not before seeing the basketball resting against the curb less than five feet away.

Not before looking over the top of the corvette's hood.

Seeing the tiny little hand resting on the pavement.

Not a twitch.

Not a tremble.

Nothing.

*Oh my God! Oh my God! Oh my God!*

*What have I done?*

*What do I do?*

*Please God no!*

His mind raced faster than he could keep up, a million thoughts bouncing and careening off of one another in a tremulous panic.

*Run*, the beast growled.

*Get in the car and drive away.*

*No*, he thought. *I can't.*

*Can I?*

He looked up in a daze, and was shocked to see all the people who had come out of their homes to see what had happened.

Saw their horrified expressions.

Their pointing fingers.

Their accusing eyes.

He watched as they grabbed their cell phones and made the three-digit phone call for help.

Panicking, Danny ran to the door of his car, the sensation in his stomach rising towards his throat, and jumped back into the driver's seat.

Fumbling for the keys, he threw the key back into the ignition.

*Do it*, the beast said, its voice growing fainter. *Drive!*

Danny felt the tears begin to slip slowly down his face, as his mind and heart struggled to serve him an answer.

In the distance, he could hear sirens.

*Life begins with driving*, he thought.

*And so it ends.*

# Better Than Dogs

*By Chris*

When the press conference finished, and her plea to the world for help had been heard, Mrs. Wix stepped down from the podium. She was replaced by Police Chief Joshua Campbell to field questions from the reporters. She was met by her husband who hugged her fiercely and then led her towards Neil and his partner Fern.

As they walked towards them Neil couldn't help but feel a slight stab of guilt run through his gut.

"We'll find your son Mrs. Wix." Neil said assuredly as they approached.

"I hope so." She replied, eyes filling with tears yet again before the ones already shed on the stage had a chance to dry up.

"I'm sure he just wandered off and got lost. Someone will spot him and give us a call."

"I hope you're right. I just….I…" Tears flowed freely down her cheeks as her husband put his arm around her shoulders and gently led her away.

"Thank you detective." Mr. Wix said as he looked over his shoulder at Neil.

Neil watched them walk away. Another family shattered. That would make eleven families in as many months. Eleven missing children, all two to three years old, and not one solid lead to go on.

"It's getting harder and harder isn't it?" His partner said from behind him.

"What's that Fern?" Asked Neil.

"Trying to tell them everything is going to be o.k. when we haven't been able to find any of the others." Frustration came through in Fern's voice.

Neil turned and looked at Fern. "We'll get this guy, and when we do, I'm going to make him wish he had never been born."

"I know we will. I just want to catch him before any more kids go missing."

"Me too buddy, me too." Neil turned and walked toward the exit of the station.

"Want to go get a drink?" Fern asked.

"No thanks, I'm going home." Neil replied tiredly. " I hear a nice hot shower calling my name."

Neil exited the building. He walked down the stairs and turned left towards the parking garage. He was tired. This case was draining him.

For almost a year now this case has been making headlines around the country. Kids missing, no leads. The police were at a standstill. They worked each scene hard, trying to find even the smallest clue or connection, but always came up empty.

The children had all gone missing from seemingly random sights. The mall, the park, their own yards. One was even taken right our of their own bed in the middle of the night.

He drove out of the garage and headed for home. Turning on the radio for the short drive, every bit of news on the radio was about the new missing boy. Andrew Wix had been taken from his back yard yesterday afternoon between the hours of four and five. The reporters were offering their opinions as to whether or not the boy would be found but the common consensus was that the boy was dead.

Neil had gotten the call at around seven yesterday about the new disappearance and headed immediately to the station where he had been ever since. It was now twenty seven hours later and he needed sleep.

By the time he got home Neil could barely keep his eyes open. All ideas of a shower were gone from his mind. He took off his shoes at the front door, walked down the hall and collapsed into bed still fully clothed.

He woke around five hours later, got out of bed and went into the kitchen. When he passed the mirror in the hall he chuckled at his disheveled appearance. He put on a pot of coffee and opened the drawer right underneath where the coffee machine stood.

Reaching into the drawer he pulled out a disposable cell phone. He looked at the phone in his hand and thought that it must have been some kind of criminal mastermind who had created the idea of these things. Absolutely untraceable, they were the perfect tool to use for breaking the law. Dialing the number for the station, he went over in his mind the tip he would call in about the missing boy.

When he hung up, he threw the phone in the trash, finished his coffee, then went and hopped into the shower.

He turned the water off in the shower to find his regular cell phone ringing in the apartment. He answered it to hear an excited Fern on the other end of the line.

"We got a break!" He said excitedly.

"Yeah?" Questioned Neil.

"Yeah, the station got a call a little while ago with some information. I'm on my way there now."

"All right." Neil replied. "I'll be there as soon as I can. I'm following up on something myself."

"What did you find?" Fern asked.

"Nothing yet. Just following a hunch. If it leads anywhere you'll be the first to know."

"All right, but if it doesn't pan out don't be long. This could be the break we need to blow this thing wide open."

Neil hung up the phone as he walked into the bedroom. He set the phone on the dresser and got dressed.

After he was dressed, he picked the phone back up and headed down into the basement. When he got to the bottom of the stairs he turned on the light. Opening a door in the left-hand wall revealed a dirty mattress on the floor inside a small room. On the mattress was the missing boy, Andrew Wix. His hands were tied behind his back.

"Andrew." Neil called.

Andrews eyes opened but he never said a word. He just looked up at Neil and began to cry.

Neil picked up the boy and led him through the door into the main room. He walked him across to another door in the opposite wall. When the door opened it revealed a large room which was cut in half by a one inch thick pane of glass. On this side of the glass was nothing but a single chair. The other side was alive with plants and trees and even a small pond.

On the left side of the glass, a door had been cut in. The door was also glass, but was locked with a latch and padlock.

Neil proceeded to unlock the door and swing it open. He grabbed Andrew and pulled him towards the door. Neil stood the boy in the doorway and untied him. When he was finished he pushed the young boy into the room, closed the door and locked it.

Andrew slowly looked around the room. He walked over and tried to push open the door as Neil sat down the chair. With the door not budging Andrew began to look around again. He moved slowly along the glass, leaving finger marks as he went.

Suddenly movement caught his eye as the plants began to spread out, opening up as some unseen thing made it's way through.

Andrew froze. When he saw the plants begin to move he panicked. He ran to the glass and began to beat on it with his little fists. He was screaming and crying now and Neil laughed out loud as a large wet spot appeared on the front of the little boys underwear.

The attack was so sudden that Neil actually jumped a bit when it happened.

The snake had struck from inside the foliage, grabbing Andrew by the arm. It jerked Andrew down and began to coil itself around him.  When the boys body was totally encompassed by it, the snake began to squeeze.

With every breath the boy exhaled the snake would squeeze even tighter. After thirty seconds the boy's face had turned a deep purple. Another minute and the snake relaxed it's grip and let go of the boys arm. It moved slowly around the body, tongue flicking in and out, tasting the air. The snake stopped when it reached the boys head.

His cell phone rang.

"Damn." He pulled it out of his pocket and looked. It was Fern. "Yeah." He said as he answered.  "Are you coming or what?" Asked Fern.

"Of course." Neil replied. "I'm on my way now." Neil hung up and turned his attention back to the snake. It had the boy's head in it's mouth and was dislocating it's own jaw to get the shoulders in.

Neil was pissed. He wanted to finish watching but he had to get to the station. He had to go and play along with this false lead. Fern was smart but Neil was just that much smarter. He has been able to manipulate the investigation any way he wanted right from the start.

Before he turned to leave he watched a second longer. The shoulders were in now. The snakes jaw and body were now working in perfect concert together and the body was going in quickly.

As he left the newspaper article on the wall caught his eye, just as it always did. Dated three years ago, the title of the article read, *SNAKE MISSING FROM ZOO.*

Looking into the enclosure again, he smiled as now only the boys legs were left sticking out of its mouth. The snake seemed to be looking right back at him.

"That's so much better than the dogs I used to feed you isn't it?"

# Thicker Than Blood

*By Chris*

"Tomorrow," Greg said.

"Are you sure you want to wait that long?" I asked.

Greg finished tossing some clothes into his suitcase. "Tomorrow should be fine." He said. "I'm only three days overdue, so if I leave in the morning I should get out OK."

"You don't really want to mess with these guys." I said trying to convince him. "You need to leave now."

"Stop worrying Bobby. I've got it all under control." He gave me one of his all knowing winks, but this time the joke is on him because everything he thought he knew was just about to go to shit.

"It's not like it is only a couple hundred bucks man. You borrowed ten thousand, and they want it back." I was starting to get desperate. "You have to get the hell out now."

I grabbed his suitcase from the bed and began making my way to the door. Greg reached out and tried to grab it from me. As we waged a foolish tug-of-war over the luggage, a loud crash came from the other room.

I let the suitcase drop from my hand and walked over to the far corner of the room. I turned to face the door while Greg stood there dumbfounded. After what seemed like an eternity, even though it was really only seconds, he came walking in.

Johnny Rocco. He was an absolute giant of a man. Standing six foot eight and built like a tank, there weren't many men who could actually look him in the eye. And for those who could, most of them just wouldn't. Everyone knew who Johnny was and what he was capable of. More than that, they all knew who he worked for.

Johnny and I were friends all throughout school. We had hung out all the time, even played on the football team together. When he started to grow to his freakishly large size though, some of the wrong people started to take notice. He even caught the eye of the worst of the bunch.

Tony Carbone.

This guy was a piece of work. Rumor had it that he once had a man killed for taking the parking space he wanted. He convinced Johnny to go and work for him, promising him money, broads, cars, and just about everything else. In the end, Johnny said yes and started being Tony's "enforcer".

Johnny had been trying for years to get me to partner up with him and I must admit, driving nice cars and having fat cash rolls did definitely hold some appeal, but I could just never see myself doing the things that I only imagined Johnny did on a daily basis.

One night Johnny came over and I had a good long talk with him, and he told me that the life wasn't everything I thought it was. He said on the rare instance that it did ever get violent, it usually ended with a couple smacks and then the person usually paid what they owed. After that talk I had gone to see Mr. Carbone the next day.

But here I stood now. In my brother's bedroom, trying to get him out of town, him being the stubborn idiot he always was, and Johnny Rocco blocking the doorway.

Johnny looked at the suitcase in Greg's hand. "Going somewhere?" He asked.

"Just going out of town tomorrow." Greg said. I could hear tremors of fear in his voice.

"You ain't been around to pay up." Johnny said taking a step towards Greg.

"I've had a hard time coming up with the money." He replied.

"Well ain't that a shame." Johnny said, opening his shirt to reveal the gun in his waistband.

"No wait!" Greg said. "I said I had a hard time coming up with it, I didn't say I don't have it."

"You have it?" Johnny asked.

"Yeah."

"Here?"

"Yeah. It's right in the nightstand." Greg dropped the suitcase on the floor and made his way over to the corner of the room where I was.

Johnny looked at me accusingly. Here I was trying to get my brother out of town, and here is my best friend trying to get to my brother. I didn't say anything. I only dropped my eyes from Johnny's gaze.

"Surprised to see you here Bobby." Johnny said.

I couldn't raise my eyes to meet his.

"I got it right here." Greg said after rifling through the end table drawer.

Johnny and I looked over to see Greg raise a gun of his own.

"Greg no!" I yelled.

I saw the muscles in Greg's arm flex, I reached out and hit his elbow as the shot rang out. It all seemed to happen in slow motion. Me hitting Greg's elbow, the gun going off, and finally watching the bullet catch Johnny right in the shoulder.

Greg spun to look at me, and when he did Johnny came forward and grabbed the gun right out of Greg's hand. He moved quickly, not like a man who had just been shot, he moved like a man who was just pissed right off. Greg turned back to look at Johnny, but Johnny was already bringing the gun around in a wide arc, connecting it with the side of Greg's head. Greg fell in a heap to the floor, unconscious.

Johnny scooped him up and slung him over his shoulders like he was nothing more than a sack of potatoes. Johnny turned and walked away.

My brother was on the shoulders of this behemoth and there I was doing nothing about it. Did I want to? Part of me did, after all, he was my brother. On the other hand, I knew my brother was a piece of shit. Not only was he never going to amount to anything, but he was always ruining the life of every person he ever met.

I followed Johnny into the other room. As I watched him walk out the door he said. "Tony wants to see you."

* * *

When I got to Tony's place half an hour later, I was let in immediately. I was ushered into his office by one of his personal bodyguards. This guy wasn't as big as Johnny, but he was still intimidating.

When I entered the office Tony was sitting behind his desk. "Come in." He said. "Have a seat."

I sat on the other side of the desk and waited. Tony seemed to be watching me carefully, almost like he was waiting for something.

"If you are waiting for me to beg for my brother's life, you're going to be waiting a long time." I told him.

A smile came across his face as he spoke.

"I take it you are not very fond of your brother." Tony said.

"Do I like him? No." I said. "But he is my brother."

"This is a tough spot you find yourself in then, yes?" He asked.

"How do you mean?"

"You came to me a while ago and asked to work for me."

"Yes."

"Well now is your chance to prove you have what it takes to be one of my men." He said as he smirked at me.

"You want me to kill my own brother?" I asked him.

"Not exactly." Tony replied. "I just want you to give him what he deserves."

"I don't follow." I said.

"Ten thousand dollars is not much in the grand scheme of things." Tony said as he stood and walked to me from behind his desk. "Is it enough to get a man killed? Who's to say?"

"Isn't that how you normally take care of things?" I questioned.

"Listen Bobby." He said as he leaned against the front of his desk. "I never take a life unless I am sure that the person has absolutely deserved it. The only thing I do is make sure that they pay one way or another."

"So what is it you want me to do?" I asked.

"I want you to be the one to make him pay."

"What like break his legs?"

"That is up to you. You'll be surprised what ten thousand dollars is worth."

"All right." I said as I stood. "How's Johnny?" I asked.

"Johnny will be fine, but that is why I need you right now." Tony smiled and led me out of the room.

* * *

When I walked into the basement room where they were holding my brother, it was like walking into something straight out of a horror movie. My brother was tied to a chair in nothing but his underwear. There was a bench along the wall only two feet away from him with just about every tool or device you can imagine might be used for hurting someone.

Greg looked up as I entered. "Bobby." He said. "Did you come to get me out of here? Did you pay him the money?"

"No, not quite." I said.

"Did you get me more time?"

"Nope."

"Then if you're not here to help me, what the hell are you doing here?"

"I've come to help Mr. Carbone collect." I said as I looked at the various tools on the bench.

"You?" Greg said in disbelief.

"Yes me." I said as Tony pulled up a chair in the far corner to watch.

"Don't do this." Greg pleaded. "Please Bobby. Just pay him and I swear I'll pay you back."

"You'll pay me back." I said as I walked over to him. "You can't get the money to pay him back, but yet you say you'll pay me back."

"Exactly Bobby, I'll get you the mon…"

His words were cut short by my fist connecting with his mouth.

"Ah shit." Greg slurred, spitting out a couple of his teeth.

"What gives you the ri…?"

I hit him again, this time crushing his nose.

"All right, all right. I've got the money."

"You do?" I asked.

"Yeah." He replied. "It's inside the middle cushion on the couch back at the apartment.

I looked over at Tony and he shook his head once and I understood what that meant. "No good." I told Greg.

"Come on Bobby. I swear on Dad's grave. The money's there."

"Dad's grave?" I asked, astonished. "Dad's grave?"

"Yeah Bobby."

"You were the one who put him in that grave, asshole." I said to him.

"What are you talking about?"

"I know that you owed money before." I said as I grabbed the pinky finger of his left hand and bent it back until I heard and felt it snap.

Greg screamed.

I waited until he stopped before I continued.

"I know you went to him and asked him for the money." I walked over to his right side now and grabbed his other pinky.

"No Bobby, please."

"Dad took out a second mortgage on his house. He gave you the money with you promising on Mom's grave to pay it back."

I snapped that finger as well.

"When you didn't pay it back, Dad lost the house." I said as I walked over to the bench with all the tools. I grabbed a chain from the bench and returned to Greg. I walked around to the back of his chair and bent down to whisper in his ear. "Do you remember how he killed himself?" I asked.

"He hung himself." Greg answered.

"That's right." I said as I stood. "He hung himself."

I had the chain in both hands. I put both arms over his head and then pulled back hard. The chain tucked up tightly around his throat and I could hear him gasping for air. I pulled hard for a few seconds then let it go.

Greg coughed and sucked in the air I had denied his lungs as I walked back over and knelt in front of him. I was about to tell him that was enough and I was letting him go now, but before I had the chance he spit in my face.

"When I get out of here, I am going to find you and kill you. Brother or not." Greg seethed.

"Kill me?"

Now I was pissed.

Kill me?"

I walked quickly over to the bench and after looking quickly I grabbed two items. I walked back over and knelt down again.

"Let's see you come get me after this." I said as I showed him one of the items I had grabbed.

It was a hammer.

I brought the hammer down eleven times. It was supposed to be ten times for ten toes but I missed once so I had to swing an extra time.

I was caught up in the moment now. Bloodlust was coursing through my veins. My hands were shaking and I was sweating but I no longer saw him as my brother. I saw him as nothing but a piece of shit that deserved everything he was getting.

I looked at his hands with the two fingers bent out of shape. I looked at his throat and saw the bruise from the chain appearing. I looked at his feet with all ten toes crushed. It wasn't enough.

The other thing I had grabbed was a straight razor. I reached out with the razor in my hand. I wrapped my arm around his legs and in one swift motion cut through both of his Achilles tendons, hobbling him.

"Let's see you come after me now." I said as I stood. I walked behind him and undid the ropes holding him to the chair.

I looked over at Tony and he was smiling.

I was just about to walk out when I heard Greg mumble something that stopped me dead in my tracks. I turned and walked back to him. I grabbed him by the hair and raised his head up.

"Say it again." I said. I was incensed.

Greg smiled.

"Fucking say it again!" I screamed in his face.

"I said maybe I can't catch you but I can still fuck your wife."

"She would never even look at a piece of shit like you." I said as I laughed.

"She already has."

I stopped laughing.

"What?" I asked.

"I said she already has."

"No way."

"I've been fucking that bitch ever since the day you got married. Why do you think she was late for the wedding? We were in the back of the limo together." Greg started to laugh. One of those laughs you expect to hear from someone who has gone mad.

"No!" I screamed.

I knocked him out of the chair and ran to the bench. My eyes focused on a baseball bat, so I grabbed it and turned back to him.

He was on his back trying to scurry away but in two strides I was next to him. I raised the bat for my swing, he raised up his arms to protect himself, and I swung with everything I had. He was mistaken. He raised his arms to protect his head but that's not what I was swinging for. The bat connected with his crotch so hard that it fell from my hands.

Greg screamed.

It was a sound I will never forget. I have never heard a scream like it since and I am not sure that I ever will. I picked up the bat again. This time I did swing for his head. The first blow knocked him unconscious but that didn't stop me. I swung until his head opened up and then I knew I was done.

I dropped the bat again and just stood there looking at what used to be my brother. Tony came walking over and stood by my side.

"Not quite what I was expecting, but a great job all the same." He said. "Let's go get you cleaned up and I'll buy you a drink."

"Actually I don't feel like a drink right now Mr. Carbone, but there is something else I would like to ask you to do for me." I said.

"Just ask and I'll see what I can do." He replied.

"Can you bring my wife down here for me?"

# Joey : Part 3

*By Chris*

My home is lonely now.

I spend a lot of time by myself and I hurt all the time.

Daddy doesn't live here anymore. I miss him. I miss the walks. Him and Mommy would get loud all the time and then one day he took a bunch of stuff and left. I still see him sometimes when he comes to get Julia, but its hard for me to walk to the door to say hi.

Now that Daddy is gone, Mommy is never home either. She is always gone in the morning and doesn't come home until late. Usually she just comes home, has a bath and goes to bed because she is very tired a lot.

I don't spend a lot of time with Julia anymore. She is always in her room now talking on her phone. Her room is upstairs and I can't get up there anymore. Sometimes she used to carry me up into her room. I would lay in the corner and she would lay on her bed. She would only talk to her friends and ignore me. Then one day she just stopped taking me up there.

Timmy still takes care of me when he is here. He can't take me for walks because I hurt now, but he feeds me and loves me still sometimes. He's not home so much anymore either. He works now to help Mommy, so he is tired sometimes too. I miss sleeping on his bed but I had a couple accidents on it so he doesn't let me up anymore.

Most days I lay here, by myself and just wait for someone to come home. My bed is under the window so I am nice and warm in the sun. My food dish is close by and so is my paper for when I need to go pee. I don't always make it to the paper but I try. I think they know that so they just clean it up and don't punish me for my accidents.

Today is a good day. I woke up and everybody was home today. I am happy. Timmy is sitting on the couch and holding me on his lap, loving me. Julia is sitting beside him and she is loving me too. She is loving me but she looks very sad. Mommy is here. She is with all of us but she looks sad too. I don't know why everyone is sad. We are all here together so we should all be happy.

Someone is knocking on the door. I used to jump and bark but I can't anymore. Now I just look. Mommy opens the door and Daddy walks in. He walks over and takes me from Timmy's lap and loves me. It's been a long time since everyone was together and I am so happy. I give lots of kisses and Daddy laughs.

Everyone is getting up and getting ready to go outside. Daddy is still holding me. They all go out the door and Daddy carries me outside. Timmy and Julia get in the back of the car. Daddy lets me go to Timmy. Daddy and Mommy get in the front.

I love car rides. It's been a long time since I went for one. I usually only go now when I go see the white-coat man. Timmy puts the window down and holds me up so I can hang my head out. The wind feels good. It makes me feel good, like I am running outside.

When the car stops I know where we are. We are going to see the white-coat man. I like him. He is very nice and I always get treats because I am a good boy. We get out and Julia looks sad again. When we are all walking in the building I reach over and give Julia a kiss, trying to make her happy. Timmy loves me as we walk in.

Usually when we come here we get to sit in the room for a while then go to another room where the white-coat man is. This time we go to a different room. I've never been in this one before. The white-coat man is here. He talks to Timmy and Timmy puts me on the table. I get ready because the white-coat man stings me every time he sees me. He always gives me a treat first so I don't mind.

Today there is no treat. Everybody is loving me now. Mommy, Daddy, Julia and Timmy. They all look sad now. I don't know why. Everyone is together. The white-coat man is here now too. Even he is loving me.

The white-coat man stings me. Now Julia and Mommy are crying. I don't understand. Daddy reaches over and loves them.

I look at Timmy. He is crying.

It's o.k. Timmy. We'll go home and I will love you.

I'm getting sleepy.

Timmy bends down and gives me a kiss on my head.

Timmy says good-bye to me.

I don't understand.

I give Timmy a kiss and go to sleep.

# The Promise

### By Chris

The long grass rolled in waves as the cool breeze blew through the night. While he walked he could feel its soothing caress and hear its whisper as it gently brushed against his legs. He held his arm out slightly as he walked, letting the palm of his hand trail along the top of the flowing blades.

*Where am I going?* He thought to himself.

Ahead of him in the distance sat what appeared to be an old cabin. The warm glow of a dim light shone through one of the windows. Jason had no idea why he was walking towards the cabin, but he knew for a fact he couldn't stop himself either.

He glanced over his shoulder to see how far he had actually come, but where there should have been a path cut in the grass from where he had been walking, there was nothing, just a continuous flow of grass. He stopped, bewildered. He looked up into the clear, starry night sky, closed his eyes and took a deep breath. As he pulled the chilly air into his lungs it felt like a thousand microscopic daggers were stabbing his insides. He held the cool air in as long as he could, until it felt as though his lungs were about to burst through his chest. He opened his eyes as he exhaled and watched his breath disappear into the night.

He turned back towards the direction he had come and tried to walk, but his feet wouldn't budge. No matter how hard he tried he could not get them to move an inch. It was as though they were encased in lead or concrete and were just too heavy to move. When he turned back towards the cabin his feet once again moved with ease.

After a few yards Jason stopped again, trying to piece together in his head what was happening to him.

\* \* \*

He remembered leaving home this afternoon. He had gotten a call from Allison, saying she was off work early and if he would mind coming to pick her up instead of her having to wait around for one of the other girls to get off and give her a ride home. He had told her no problem. It had always made him happy when she got off early because it meant that he got to spend extra time with her.

He waited for her in the casino parking lot and tried not to think about the things he saw, but also the things he couldn't see. He still wished to this day that he could go back inside, see the lights, hear the sounds and feel how he used to feel when he was allowed inside.

The promise.

That's what kept him outside. That's what kept him dreaming of the inside. It's not that he wasn't allowed back inside, he was able to go in at any time he pleased, but to do so could cost him everything he held dear.

* * *

There was a time in the not so distant past when he used to go in. He used to hold the chips. He used to hold the cards. He used to call "all in". But most of all he used to win.

Not so long ago, people knew who he was. When he sat at a table you could almost hear an audible groan from the other players. He was a champion and people knew it. Sometimes the younger, cockier guys trying to make a name for themselves would come and sit at his table intentionally, just hoping against hope that they could be the one to knock the mighty Jason Hamel out of the game. They came, they played, and they left the table pouting like a six year old who was just scolded for getting his clothes dirty.

He had gone on a run like nothing that had ever been done before. Then one day it all just fell apart. He had made more money in two months playing poker than most people manage to make in ten years of working, but one loss was all it took.

One loss and the winning streak he was on ended in an instant. In a matter of weeks he was entering every possible tournament he could, trying to recapture the confidence that would bring the money and the fame. But the wins never came again.

It had gotten to the point where the bank accounts were empty and the lines of credit were maxed. When it finally came to her attention what he was doing, Allison sat him down and talked to him for a while. At first she was rational and calm, then she got angry and was yelling for a while. She never did cry though. She was a tough one, he had to give her credit for that.

At the end of it all she had walked away and left him with the ultimatum, either stop playing poker and get a normal job or she was leaving and taking the kid with her.

Nathan.

He couldn't let her take him away. Nathan was his world and when she threatened him with not seeing his child his mind had been made up in an instant.

The feeling he would get when he would win at cards still paled in comparison to the feeling he would get when he would come home and hold his baby boy.

He wound up getting a job cleaning offices at night. It was actually quite ideal because it left the days open for Allison to go and work during the day, and they would never have to worry about childcare. He had never guessed that she would wind up getting a job at the one place she didn't want him to be. Maybe it was her way of making sure he would never go back inside.

Not that she had to worry about it anyway. He prided himself on being a man of his word, and when he told her that he was going to stop gambling, he had meant every word. Sticking to that promise had given him back everything that he almost lost.

\* \* \*

He remembers she had come out the doors of the casino, and smiled at him when she saw that he was already there waiting. She climbed into the truck and leaned over and gave him a kiss.

"Thanks for coming baby," she said as she pulled the seatbelt over her shoulder and latched it into place. "Where's Nathan?"

"Your mother was over so she's sitting with him 'til we get home," he replied as he put the truck in gear and pulled away.

"That must have been torture for you. Having her over," she chided.

He chuckled. "You know I don't mind your mother, besides it gave me a chance to go out and clean the garage."

They drove along, gabbing nonchalantly about the goings on of the day. There were some silences, but they weren't the awkward silences you get when there's tension in the air. No, they were the silences you get when you enjoy each other's company so much you don't need to say anything.

\* \* \*

Standing here in this unknown field it was all playing out like a movie in front of his eyes.

\* \* \*

She had asked him something and he had glanced over at her to reply and that was when the crash came.

There had been a motorcycle coming down the road at a high rate of speed and for some unknown reason it had veered into their lane and collided with them head on. The collision sent the bike flying over top of the truck, landing in a heap of grinding metal and plastic on the pavement about thirty yards away. The rider of the bike came through the truck windshield, colliding with Jason.

\* \* \*

Suddenly the visions were gone and he was left standing alone in the strange field, and that was when the certainty hit him.

*I'm dead.*

It hit him like a giant weight causing his knees to buckle and he fell to the ground crying. He had to fight hard to resist the urge to vomit as the convulsions from crying shook his body to it's core. After a while he found the strength to get back to his feet and regain some composure.

He looked around and thought for a moment. If he was dead, what was this place?

*Was this heaven?*

It wasn't what heaven had been pictured like in his mind. He had always thought of it as angels, clouds and singing. If it wasn't heaven, what was it then?

*Hell?*

But again the mental picture of hell didn't suit the situation either. Where were the demons, where was the fire? The brimstone?

*No.*

*This was something else.*

He had heard talk before of a place people called Limbo. Is that where he was? Was he doomed to walk through this strange field forever, or was there more to this than what he could actually see? He was sure the cabin had something to do with it, so he started walking quicker than before and set out towards the cabin.

As he approached, a feeling of dread washed over him. It was so overwhelming that he had the urge to turn and run away as fast as he could but he knew that even if he tried he wouldn't be able to get anywhere.

He didn't want to get any closer. He just stood ten or so yards away from the building, waiting for something, anything that would help him get away from here.

Somehow he knew that he could stand here forever and things would just remain as they are. He also knew for a fact that it was important that he go inside. Steeling his courage, deciding he really had nothing to lose, he took a few tentative steps forward.

When he got closer to the cabin he could see that it was a rickety old building, it looked almost ancient. The boards had shrunk over time and there were gaps in the walls where he could see a dim light shining through. He reached out to open the door as he approached but the door swung inward slowly just out of reach. He climbed the three steps to get inside and stepped into the room.

Once inside he took a quick look around to survey the interior. Across the room there were two closed doors. In the middle of the room stood an old table with two chairs, on the table was what appeared to be an oil lamp, and sitting in one of the chairs was what appeared to be a middle aged man. Jason took a step forward and the door he came in slowly closed behind him.

"Welcome," said the man. His voice was soft, almost soothing.

"Who are you?" Jason asked.

"It doesn't matter who I am," the man replied. "Have a seat."

"I think I'd rather stand." Jason said as he backed away a step from the table.

"No really, I insist," said the man.

Suddenly the empty chair spun around on it's own to face him. When it did, Jason turned around and reached for the knob of the door he had entered through, but the door was gone.

"WHAT'S GOING ON HERE?" Jason screamed as he turned to face the other man.

"Everything will be explained to you when you sit down." A note of sternness had now entered into the strange man's voice. Suddenly Jason had the feeling this was a man to be feared.

Jason walked back over to the table and reluctantly sat down.

"Listen," started Jason. "I don't know why it is I am here, or what any of this is about…"

"Relax." There was that soothing voice again. "I will answer all your questions under one condition."

"What's that?" Asked Jason.

"After you are satisfied with your answers, you play a game with me."

"Game?" Questioned Jason. "What kind of game?"

"First, your questions."

"Alright." Jason thought for a moment, agitated. He studied the other man's face. He had become very good at reading people, but this man's face seemed to be etched in stone. Not a muscle moved, no nervous tic, as far as Jason could tell the man didn't even blink.

"First off, what should I call you? Creepy guy with the soothing voice might not go over so well." Jason joked.

"You can call me…" The man paused. "Stan."

No smile. No smirk. Not even a hint of emotion.

"Alright Stan, how many questions am I allowed to have?"

"You may have as many as you like until you are satisfied and are ready to play."

"Yeah, that's right. A game." Jason said sarcastically. "All right, so what is this place?"

"It's a cabin." Stan replied without even giving off the hint of a smile.

Jason suddenly stood up quickly, sending the chair sliding backwards against the wall with the back of his knees. He rushed to the other side of the table, bent down and screamed at Stan. *"IS THIS SOME KIND OF SICK JOKE TO YOU?"*

"No, it is not." Stan replied, still showing no emotion.

Jason reached out to grab Stan by the throat but when his hands got to within a few inches of the bare flesh under his chin, they were stopped by some unseen force. Jason could feel heat coming from the man's skin. It was a heat that no human being could possibly live with. Jason pulled his hands away quickly when they felt hot enough to burn. Jason tried again, so hard that his hands shook, but again he was denied the grip he so badly wanted.

*"AAAAHHHH!"* Jason screamed as he turned away.

He began wildly pacing the room. All the while staring at Stan, who still only sat in the chair looking like a statue. After a few moments he slowed, and began taking deep breaths to calm himself. When at last he felt like he was relaxed enough, Jason walked over, slid the chair back to the table and sat down. He looked at Stan in all his emotionless glory and asked Stan another question. "Is this Heaven?"

"No."

"Is this Hell?"

"No."

"Is this umm… Limbo?"

"No."

Jason had to calm himself before frustration could set back in. He looked over at Stan who just looked back, patiently waiting. The man was a rock. Jason thought carefully before asking his next question.

"What is this plane of existence that we are in right now?" He finally asked.

"We are in what is called a Void."

"*FINALLY!* Now we're getting somewhere." Jason exclaimed. "Does this mean I am dead?"

"No."

"I'm not dead?"

"No."

Jason was baffled.

"Why am I here, in this Void?"

"This is where we decide if we are going to let you go back."

"Back where?" Jason asked.

"To your body."

"I'm sitting right here, pretty sure I'm in my body."

"No you are not."

"All right I'll play along. Where is my body?" Jason asked, clearly agitated again.

"Your physical body lies in a hospital bed."

"In a hospital bed?"

"Yes." Stan replied.

"Why is my body in a hospital bed?"

"You are in a coma."

Jason was dumbfounded. For a moment he couldn't speak. He could only conjure pictures of himself lying motionless in a bed, with tubes coming out of his nose and mouth. Snapping back to the moment, he asked. "Is this what everyone who is in a coma goes through?"

"Yes. There were many before you, and there will be many after."

"What is the purpose of this Void?" Jason asked.

"This is where the decision is made as to whether you wake up or not."

"How is that decided?" Jason asked as he got up from his seat and began to pace again.

"The game."

"I have to win a game to live?" Jason asked.

"No."

"What then?"

"All you have to do is play and the decision will be made."

Jason stopped pacing. A look of worry washed over his face, he turned to Stan. "Is Allison OK?"

"She is fine."

The worry washed away as fast as it appeared. Jason walked back over, pulled the chair closer to the table and sat back down. "How do I get out of here?"

"Through one of the two doors behind me."

"Where do they lead?"

"One leads back to your body, and the other leads to the afterlife."

"How do I know which one to open?"

"You don't. One will open for you."

"When?"

"When you play the game."

"So what's this ga…"

Before he could finish Jason looked down and discovered that the table had changed from the old one he first saw when he walked in, to a brand new poker table.

Jason again suddenly shot up from his seat. "I can't." He stammered. "I can't play that game."

"Sure you can," said Stan.

"No," Jason said, sitting back down and lowering his head into his hands.

Behind his hands Jason could hear the soft whisper of cards sliding across the table and coming to a stop in front of him. Jason lowered his hands and looked at Stan.

"I can't do this."

"Sure you can," Stan replied.

"No I can't." Thoughts ran through Jason's head at a pace where they began to become jumbled.

"Yes you can." Stan said, but this time there was a hard edge to his voice.

Stan picked up the two cards in front of him, looked at them, and then placed them back on the table.

Jason looked down at the two cards laying face down in front of him.

"Here, let me help you." Stan said.

The cards began to slowly slide closer to Jason's hand.

"NO!" Jason yelled, again jumping to his feet.

The cards stopped moving and as Jason looked at Stan he could see a flash of anger across the man's face.

"Sit down Jason, and play the game with me." Stan said, regaining his composure.

"No, I won't." This time Jason was wearing the mask of stone as he stood in front of the table.

"Sit down and play the game with me," Stan repeated.

Jason could see something in the man's face. Like his face was nothing more than a mask, and there was another, horrible face hidden underneath.

"No."

"SIT YOUR ASS DOWN AND PLAY!" Stan screamed as he got to his feet. He leaned on the table with both arms. Jason could swear that he heard the wood crack under his grip.

Jason walked over and leaned on his side of the table, bringing his face close to Stan's. The heat was emanating off Stan's skin hotter than before. "No," he said, as calm as ever.

Stan screamed.

It was a scream like no human being was ever meant to hear. A sound that no human being could possibly make. Jason squeezed his eyes tight and covered his ears the best he could to drown out the sound.

When the scream was finished, Jason lowered his hands and opened his eyes.

Stan was gone.

The cards were gone.

The table and chairs were gone.

Jason hoped he had figured it out right. To play the game was death. He had been living his life based on an agreement between himself and Allison, and to break that agreement would mean his end, even in this place.

Jason looked across the room and one of the two doors was now open to reveal only blackness. He walked across the room and peered inside. He could see nothing. The darkness was total.

Taking a deep breath he slowly stepped inside.

\* \* \*

Allison was drifting off to sleep in her chair by the hospital bed when her thoughts were suddenly interrupted by a whispering of unintelligible sounds. It was the same pattern repeating itself over and over.

She opened her eyes and almost screamed when she saw Jason's eyes open and staring right at her. He was trying to say something to her. She jumped out of her chair. "Hold on baby, I'm going to go get the doctor. I love you." With that she ran out of the room.

Jason's eyes followed her as she left the room. Just as she turned out of sight he whispered, "I kept my promise."